FOOTBALL
FUSSBALL
VOETBAL

Colin Cameron is a specialist sports writer. He graduated from Christ's College, Cambridge in 1986 with a degree in Political Economy and has subsequently contributed to a wide cross-section of newspapers and magazines on sport and related issues. This is his third book. He has also written: *The Contenders* on athletics, and *Ryan Giggs Soccer Skills* with Ryan Giggs and Sir Bobby Charlton.

FOOTBALL FUSSBALL VOETBAL

THE EUROPEAN GAME 1956-EURO96

Colin Cameron

BBC BOOKS

To Freddie Dakin
and all other future followers of European football

ACKNOWLEDGEMENTS

There would have been no *Football, Fussball, Voetbal* without the help of
others. A large debt of gratitude is owed to everyone who assisted in any way
towards the book's publication. Thanks is due in particular, to Julian Flanders of
BBC Books, for his patience and professionalism, to Patrick Walsh of the
Christopher Little Literary Agency, for his shuttle diplomacy, to Niall Sloane of
BBC Sport, for his sympathetic consideration of the manuscript and gentle
correction of the author's many misconceptions, to Mike Penson of the BBC,
for his tolerance of the many seemingly irrelevant requests for video footage,
to Hugh Jones for allowing his vast linguistic and footballing reservoir of
knowledge to be at least partially tapped, to Liz Eddison for photographs, to
Emma Tait, and to all who gave up their time to be interviewed. There would
also have been no book without the sanity provided by those who are usually
found south of the river (or in the cinema) who were unilaterally
commandeered to supply the author with unwarranted sympathy during the
manuscript's completion.

Published by BBC Books,
an imprint of BBC Worldwide Publishing.
BBC Worldwide Limited, Woodlands,
80 Wood Lane, London W12 0TT

First published 1995
© Colin Cameron 1995
The moral right of the author has been asserted

ISBN 0 563 38714 9

Set in Gill Sans Light 11½/ 17pt
Design and typeset by Grahame Dudley Associates
Printed and bound in Great Britain by BPC Paulton Books Ltd., Paulton Nr Bristol
Colour separations by Radstock Repro Ltd., Midsomer Norton, Somerset
Cover printed by Clays Ltd., St Ives plc

CONTENTS

INTRODUCTION

Somewhere in Europe there is a library big enough to contain a complete and comprehensive history of continental football. What a room that must be. Filled with volumes: books on every European club, including those now defunct; notes on every game, even those that were intolerably dull; details of every stadium, the newest arenas, those that today heave with the emotions of the spectators they house, and also those that now shame their proud history, having fallen into disrepair. The last inclusion would remind us of great days. The library would, in time, also serve as a durable monument to the past exploits of Di Stefano and the great Real Madrid side of the 1950s, to the Italian giants of the 1960s, to those who perished at Munich, in the Superga plane crash and at Heysel, to treble Champions Cup winners of the seventies Ajax and Bayern Munich, to Liverpool, to the French of 1984, to the Milan of the nineties, and to many others who have excelled on the European stage in years gone by and who will excel in the future.

If such a library existed, *Football, Fussball, Voetbal* would serve as an introduction for those fascinated by the continental game and poised to venture into its real history for the first time. In attempting to cover 40 years of European football, the book omits the odd moment of significance and individuals of importance for sure. Nevertheless, the essence of European football – the spirit, the recurring themes, the unique national significance of the continental game to each country – over the first four decades in Spain, Italy, Britain, the Netherlands, Germany, France and the rest of the mainland is contained in the pages of this book.

The words will also help put in context the forthcoming European Championships to be held in England in 1996. The section in our imaginary European football library devoted to this competition would not, in truth, take up much floor space as most of the nine previous tournaments do little justice to what has evolved since the inaugural staging in 1960. But if you are lucky enough to attend any of the 31 matches of Euro96, your enjoyment may be enhanced by the possession of the information contained here that explains why the tenth Championships is the most significant of the series to date.

Having been denied European club football for five long years, between 1985 and 1990, the British game is today perhaps more aware of the joys of the European game than any other nation. England will prove an enthusiastic host to the continent's latest international gathering. Her clubs will also be eager participants, too, in future Champions, Cup Winners' and UEFA Cup tournaments, while this denial is still fresh in the mind.

This book will hopefully stir recollections of greatness from the past and set the scene for the future. It will also explain what European football means to our continental cousins, why it is important everywhere to succeed beyond the boundaries of the domestic game, why this goal is the only way club sides can achieve true greatness in the footballing world. Why after 40 glorious years, European football, fussball, voetbal, call it what you will, matters so much to so many.

Colin Cameron,
London, 1995.

SPAIN AND PORTUGAL

THE GOAL OF GREATNESS

Real Madrid, winners of the first five European Cups and the continent's inaugural champions of champions. They set the standard of excellence for European Cup football.

For the fans of Real Madrid, it had been a long wait. To win, at last, a European Champions Cup Final, ending the suffering of supporters who had been raised on the great Real teams from the past only to see their heirs to a tradition repeatedly fail to meet the ultimate club challenge, was to end years of anguish. Children present for the occasion – bless those budding little Di Stefanos – would no longer have to look back at times before they were born to find their heroes. Black and white prints and grainy television footage could be replaced with glorious Technicolour and crystal-clear video tape recording. In April, 1995, a new dawn broke over Spain's capital city. Birds sang in the trees that line the impressive boulevards leading to the magnificent Bernabeu Stadium. Some even whispered that the 5,500 trophies housed there had a special glint by daybreak, the same glint found in the eyes of fans from the 1950s when their gaze fixed on the white, the pure white, of Real Madrid.

Well, sort of. At least, reading some reports, the occasion could have been a football match. A Spanish official remarked of the final played in Zaragoza against Olympiakos from Greece: 'The police confiscated chains, sticks, and some drugs, hashish. One of the fans was carrying a loaded shotgun.' A motorway service station riot – where shots were fired – added to the modern footballing feel. There is, it seems, some corner of a foreign land that is forever England, and in April it was Zaragoza.

Alas, though, for football fans of Real, it was merely basketball honour at stake. Success in the Champions Cup in a discipline where a dribble requires a bounce as well as verve did finally come for the club after a 15-year drought with a 73-61 win over the visiting Greeks. But for followers of the more beautiful game, another year had passed in pursuit of a seventh European Cup victory, a first since 1966. At six-foot plus, Real's top scorer, Arvidas Sabonis, was, in truth, always an unlikely replacement in the sporting hearts of Spain's capital for the divine Alfredo Di Stefano. For a true successor to the city's impresario of the round ball, the citizens would have to wait another year at least.

Like the history of Real Madrid, European club football is dominated by the European Champions Cup. Of course, for almost as many years as the European Cup has been in existence, there has been opportunity for success on the same stage in European football's two other great challenges, the Cup Winners' Cup and the UEFA Cup. That has been the case since the former was first staged in 1960/61 and the latter – which began life in 1955 as the Inter Cities Fairs Cup for exactly that, cities hosting fairs – evolved into its current form, a Euro-consolation prize for domestic league near-misses. But all over the continent and Britain, particularly in Manchester and Glasgow, the Champions Cup is all. And nowhere more so than in Spain.

It was club President Santiago Bernabeu, the spiritual father of Real and in the 1920s also its centre forward, who first fully devoted himself and Real's resources to the pursuit of a competition that he deemed worthy of the team he was building and the stadium, now bearing his name, that he had already built. Indifference from some in authority not withstanding – Chelsea were declined the opportunity to compete in the first tournament of 1955/56 by a short-sighted Football League – the competition began with a 16-club entry, some not even domestic champions, and ended with a happy result for Bernabeu, a win for Real. And a happy result it ultimately proved, too, for the rest of Europe, establishing as it did a true test of greatness. Success in the European Cup is now a prerequisite for any club aiming acquire the hallmark of greatness. Real's five consecutive victories from 1956, culminating in a glorious triumph in 1960, both confirmed them as one of the great club teams of all time and established the European Cup as the standard for the future.

Only a great side could have achieved such a sweep and only such a team could have gifted the infant tournament the necessary kudos it needed to become a fixture at a stroke. Without Real, the European Cup could have floundered like a ZDS, a Texaco, an Anglo-Italian or a Watney's. A Carling Premiership lager toast to Real is in order every time you tune in to *Trevor Brooking's European Football Night* on Radio 5 Live, as well as thanks that everyone has ultimately profited from the mutually beneficial relationship instantly enjoyed between Real Madrid and the European Cup.

In Spain, around one in four people support Real Madrid. Conversely, three in four hate them. The ratio is even less favourable to Real – and even more polarised – in Catalonia. In the past, when Franco joined the throng in the

Bernabeu – for it was he who ultimately ensured Di Stefano's permanent presence in the stadium, or so they say – the three were less vocal than the one, but the dissenters found their voice with the autocrat's death in 1975. How they cheer today, when Real lose.

Thoughts of politics aside, if there is a domestic comparison to be drawn between Real and an English side, only Manchester United fit the bill. The ratio of admirers to carpers may be different, but the principles of division are the same; the arrogance and ebullient self-confidence of those who perceive themselves as the best (no pun intended on George) by right provokes loathing of the worst kind.

In Real's case, certainly in the early days, the harbouring of illusions of grandeur were not matched by the club's achievements – and most definitely not by its facilities – and this combination of conceit unsupported by results, did little to endear them to arch rivals, near and far. The workers of Madrid preferred to follow Atlético, the mattress makers with club origins in the factories of the city. The idle rich, meanwhile, adopted Real. Even before the regal prefix (Real means Royal in Spanish) was bestowed on the club, it declined to employ professionals as players, nor to compete in the Spanish league until the 1920s adding weight to accusations of sporting snobbery. The Corinthian philosophy did not mean that Real possessed a great deal of the modesty usually found in the amateur game, either. The all white of Madrid was, itself, something of an arrogant statement. Is it, three quarters of Spain asks, a practical colour for a football kit? Many a Yorkshire mother will tell you otherwise.

But for Santiago Bernabeu, the belief that he was part of the best wasn't enough. He had to prove it, too. After becoming club President in 1943, he began to devise a plan to dominate the paid professionals and kick start the club into achieving the status it now enjoys in the hearts of at least a quarter of the population as Spain's glamour club. A Kevin Costner before his time, Bernabeu first proposed to address the aesthetics and construct a stadium on the club's present site that would have a cathedral-style quality – a sort of 'Field of Dreams'. Like the screen star's baseball-obsessed character he believed that 'if he built it, they would come'. He was right. They did. And what's more, they paid for it in bonds snapped up when the extent of Bernabeu's dream for the then-

Santiago Bernabeu, the spiritual father of Real Madrid, embraced the European Cup as an opportunity for his club to achieve greatness that stretched beyond Spanish borders. By 1960, his ambitions were comprehensively fulfilled.

modest Chamartín site, home to a mere 16,000 fans in those days compared with the six-figure crowds of today, became known.

Players, too, were bought with the cash. And only the best. Bernabeu paid for them with an urgency predating but no less compulsive than Jack Walker's appetite for class at Blackburn. The likes of Kopa, who performed for Reims in the first European Cup Final against Real was swiftly recruited after defeat. The policy had something of a six-pointer quality about it; we want the best and we also want to avoid playing against the best of the rest if we can. Very Italian. Similar thoughts, perhaps, to those in the back of Alex Ferguson's mind when he bought Andy Cole.

But Spain was one thing. Bernabeu had even wider hopes for Real. By the 1950s, the result of his industry was an outstanding team. Along with the quality rose the need for a greater challenge than the Spanish League afforded. Hence Bernabeu's desire to see a competition established to frank the greatness of his creation, and his wholehearted support of the European Cup concept. A hurried birth was induced to bring into the world of football a test, cobbled together, to crown one domestic championship team as rulers of a continent.

That Real, in this their heyday, warranted the status was beyond dispute. Real were deservedly kings of Europe. And the final coronation came in Glasgow in 1960. Prior to that, Real had already won the first four European Cups, itself an incredible achievement, and some great players had been and gone. Nevertheless, their accomplishments seemed even more substantial after THAT thrilling encounter with Eintracht Frankfurt. The symbiotic quality of Real's relationship with the European Cup was confirmed that May night. A great team won a competition it had itself made great. It was the occasion for the first European toast, albeit predating a then teenage Trevor Brooking yet to make his mark on our airwaves, but deserved nonetheless.

When Real came to Scotland for their fourth defence of the European Cup, they were the best club side in the world. Television had granted them substantial recognition — all four previous Finals had been screened — earning them more fame than any of their footballing predecessors, and following on from the Mighty Magyars, Hungary's supremely gifted international side of the 1950s, they went a long way to ending football insularity in Europe.

Kenneth Wolstenholme was at the European microphone while much of this mould breaking was taking place. He remembers: 'Everybody wanted to see them. They could fill any ground in England. They made the European Cup in its first five years and deserve recognition for being the catalyst in establishing it so quickly as the supreme goal in European football. The televised Finals captured the imagination. We had had our isolationist blinkers removed by a bunch of Hungarians who came from a strange place where they staged comic operas and Real and their European Cup successes came on that swell. We suddenly knew what continental football was all about.

'They had fabulous players. Bernabeu was a father figure like Jack Walker. He didn't really want the publicity but agreed to be president and just asked how much the club needed for the best players. He just said he wanted the best. The team had fabulous stars. They might have struggled with the three foreigners rule of today, but in fact they would have just changed the nationalities. They didn't really worry about defence. Theirs was a Brazilian attitude. They thought they

would score more than they would concede.' They usually did.

That Real had great players was beyond all reasonable argument. By the time 1960 arrived, Di Stefano had been joined by Puskas and although Kopa had departed, back to France, the likes of Paco Gento, one of the fastest wingers in the history of the game, remained. Indeed, the Real European Cup Final team of 1960 is remembered off pat by a generation of schoolboys, the true eleven times table of its day; Dominguez, Marquitos, Pachin, Vidal, Santamaria, Zarraga, Canario, Del Sol, Di Stefano, Puskas, Gento.

Di Stefano was the heart and soul of Real. He played as a deep-lying centre forward, although few recognised the concept in those days. He had joined Real from Colombian football outright, only after the seemingly inevitable dispute — few transfers in the Mediterranean are straightforward — over who had signed the balding Argentine whose jutting jaw and regal pose made him a natural to

(Left to right) Del Sol, Di Stefano, Puskas, and Gento, four of the great Real Madrid side who combined to set a standard of excellence in Europe for others to emulate. Together they left an indelible imprint on many a schoolboy's mind.

15

play in the white robes of Real. Not so said Barcelona, who also claimed to have signed him. And on arriving in Spain, Di Stefano began his European career with the intention of alternating between Barça and Real from season to season as both clubs' lawyers claimed to have bought and brought the player from South America.

There are two versions as to what happened next. The first suggests that President Franco intervened. Di Stefano was to play for Real, whom he worshiped, and that was that. Barça would have to sell any notional stake they had in him. The second maintains that this sharing arrangement was agreed, but Di

Alfredo Di
Stefano, the
heart and soul of
Real Madrid,
with regal looks
and poise to
match his status.

Stefano started rather badly for Real and Barça lost interest and agreed to sell him. Strangely, within 24 hours of the deal, Di Stefano returned to his best form orchestrating a 5-0 thrashing of Barça by Real, scoring four himself. As a prelude to Maurice Johnston's shenanigans with Rangers and Celtic, this is hard to match.

In Di Stefano's formative years, his farming father had noted little Alfredo's abilities with the ball and warned his mother, anxious that son and heir should follow into the family trade, that no one would be banished to a football-free agricultural wilderness. Papa Di Stefano concluded of his son's future: 'He can't play football with the cattle.'

How shrewd. Di Stefano was the conductor, Real's all-stars his instruments. The music was up-tempo and the sound rich and resonant. Not everyone hit the right note. The great Brazilian Didi — whose free kicks were said to drop like falling leaves under the bar and into the net — came to Real but never managed to find a role for himself in the all-white. Described once as having the 'remotely brooding aspect of a great Negro jazz musician', Didi was never allowed to fit into Di Stefano's classically orientated footballing orchestra. The heart of Real, it seemed, was not interested in soul. Didi left after one season, probably because his skills too closely duplicated those of Di Stefano.

But there was room for others. Even Di Stefano accepted that he needed colleagues, occasionally. Puskas for one was wholly embraced. In fact, the great Hungarian, known outside Spain as the Galloping Major but to his family as Ocsi (little brother, although by the time he joined Real he was far from little) was the perfect foil to Di Stefano. Having spent a period in footballing quarantine with Milan, a consequence of seeking political asylum from the uncertainty of his troubled native land, Puskas was soon scoring with his internationally renowned left foot in glorious harmony with Di Stefano the provider. Real were benefiting from the care Puskas showed as a child in protecting his one shoe, all his father could afford, which fitted his right foot the best.

Wolstenholme remembers: 'People say Puskas was one-footed but he had a good right foot if all he did was stand on it. He could hit long shots, but he was always around for the tap-ins, a bit like Jimmy Greaves. He was an out-and-out goalscorer, he'd never come back for the ball and spray it around. He complemented Di Stefano beautifully.'

Complimented, too. In his first season for Real, Puskas was neck and neck with Di Stefano to be Spain's leading goalscorer, but in the last game of the season, Puskas rounded the keeper only to pass the ball across the open goal to his team-mate when it was easier to score. The gesture struck a chord with the maestro as he buried it into the net. Di Stefano would yield to this man. There was room in Real for one more star, even for Pancho as the portly Puskas was later called in Spain.

Today Puskas reflects that the game is now very defensive: 'You lose a match and the following week the people do not come to watch. It is mostly a technical problem. The players, years ago, didn't play defensive football, they knew their jobs.' Di Stefano's to create, Puskas' to score. Wolstenholme reflects: 'They (a South American and a Hungarian) didn't speak each other's language, but they understood. There is a football language that great players speak and if you don't speak it, you are not a great player.'

That much we can all grasp.

For many, including Wolstenholme who commentated, the game in Glasgow for the fifth European Cup was the greatest ever seen. Indeed, Glasgow was a great choice of venue. And not just because Hampden Park had room for 138,000. Eintracht Frankfurt had scored 12 against Rangers over the two legs of the semi-final and, as a result, alliances, both strong and unusual, emerged. Celtic's papalists united to a man behind the Germans with all Glasgow's protestants firmly behind the Spanish church's finest. The city was completely polarised. It was ever thus, although on this occasion, the divisions temporarily reversed the usual sectarian battle lines.

The players were on £650 to win, plus, of course, a gold winner's medal. They were, as Wolstenholme announced to the watching nation, the greatest club side the world had ever seen. What's more, they had displaced that great figure of television mystery at the time, Koran, whose usual invitation to a half hour of intrigue was withdrawn by the BBC to make space for the match. 'Koran always seems to know everything,' Wolstenholme mused on air. 'But he didn't know he would not be on television tonight.' Real's powers, it seemed had no bounds.

A more pertinent mystery than Koran's unscreened quest remains unsolved

to this day; how Frankfurt were so comprehensively beaten. Wolstenholme maintains: 'Anyone who could score 12 goals in two games against Rangers must have been a good side and they were. I don't think I have ever seen a side play so well and get beaten so comfortably. They were terribly unlucky to catch Real on such a day. They have never been in the European Cup Final since. In fact, I don't think they have excelled in Germany either. The whole thing must have been quite a shock.'

Certainly it began with a surprise. The Germans took the lead. Big mistake. Stirred Real were brilliant, no one more so than Gento on the left wing. To the full house that gathered for the game at Hampden, his display of flicks and dummies, back heels and trickery, thrilled an audience more than familiar with the joy of wing play. There was no malice or tactical cynicism, either. The first offside decision came after a free-flowing 70 minutes: 'Some of the exponents of the offside

Di Stefano slides the ball home against Eintracht Frankfurt in 1960, completing a 7-3 triumph. Hampden Park acclaimed one of the greatest team performances ever and Glasgow lined the route back to the city from the ground to acknowledge the style of Real's fifth European Cup success.

19

game as their only contribution to soccer will be scratching their heads', remarked Wolstenholme. Notable also was the desire of Real. With the game won at 3-1, they were awarded a penalty. Puskas hungrily grabbed the ball for the strike. The team knew they were champions and wanted to win like champions. And so they did, 7-3.

It is a frequent shortcoming of many modern stadiums that they don't possess a facility that enables winners to receive their trophies and rewards in full view of the spectators. Hampden in 1960 could only offer the heroes of Madrid a table and with it an elevation that was modest compared with the footballing heights they had reached on the field. It did not satisfy the crowd. Wolstenholme remembers: 'Real got the trophy and must have thought, very good, it hasn't changed much since we last had it, and then went to their dressing-room. But the crowd were still chanting for them. In the end they had to come out and do a lap of honour. By this time some players were in bare feet.' Outside the stadium, the adulation continued. The roads were lined with people who cheered equally both teams. A standard had been vividly set and handsomely acclaimed.

In 1960, the first European Nations' Cup Final also took place. At least, that is what the record books tell us. You would struggle to find anyone who remembers it with great fondness. Apart, that is, from the inaugural winners, the old Soviet Union, successful after extra time by the odd goal in three against the then Yugoslavia. With both representatives having ceased to feature prominently in geography lessons, it seems unlikely that the year will hold as much significance for the once-every-four-years tournament as 1960 did for its sister club contest. Occurrences of note? Lev Yashin apparently had a good game. Another curiosity is that the referee was England's Arthur Ellis (Britain at the forefront of emerging Europe?). But it was a further 20 years before the competition, having been gifted the grander title of the European Championships, became worthy even of World-Cup-style finals, the five previous tournaments warranting only two-legged knockout rounds up to the semi-final stages when four teams gathered for a modest affair in one country. Like the European Cup, the Nations Cup needed a great team to win it for credibility. It got it in 1984, but in 1960, Platini's finest hour for France was a long way off.

Spain played her part in the beginning, though, both by making up the numbers and by cementing the ties that bind sport and politics. President Franco, whose interest in football didn't extend beyond the city walls of Madrid except for internationals, scratched Spain from the first tournament after they were drawn to play the Soviet Union. Their support for the socialists during the Spanish Civil War was not acceptable to him. With the team Spain could have fielded, it was a great opportunity, unusually missed by the General, to score – literally – many propaganda points over any remaining dissenters to his rule.

A similar opportunity presented itself four years later, but this time it was grasped. Spain actually won the second Nations Cup in 1964 defeating the Soviets 2-1. A decisive, if uninspired, victory was secured in front of Franco and 120,000 others in the Bernabeu. A rare victory for fascism in Europe, but also a muted one. The red flag was lowered that day by a Spanish team devoid of creative ideas and an instinct for goal. The starting line-up for the Spanish national team that day: Iribar, Rivilla, Calleja, Fuste, Olivella, Zoco, Amancio, Pereda, Marcelino, Suarez, Lapetra, hardly rolls off the tongue in the same way as great Real side of four years before.

The Spaniards would have cause to regret abandoning their instinct for flair. If they had known then that their national side was destined to underachieve for the next 30 years, they might have attempted to perform with the style synonymous with Real in the hope that the Nations Cup would be acknowledged as equal to the European Cup as a mark of greatness. In reality, local rivalry was granted a higher priority.

It is a recurring lament. Many blame this passion and the divided nature of Spanish society for its international shortcomings. The Catalans are suspected of being reluctant to pass to those who usually wear the dictatorial white of Madrid, and vice versa, even when all are sporting the same coloured Spanish shirt. This certainly makes it hard for a manager to get the best team results from individuals certainly gifted enough to achieve success within Europe.

Indeed, breaching the Barcelona-Madrid discord has proved beyond both the great and the good. Even a nationally revered figure like Di Stefano, whose abilities and Argentine nationality allowed a wider admiration than might otherwise have been permitted for someone synonymous with Madrid, carried little clout

Despite having players of the calibre of Emilio Butragueno, Spain have disappointed in the European Championships since their home victory in 1964.

21

(Right) The trophy room at the Bernabeu Stadium sparkles with history. *(Below)* Today, the ground fills with supporters, proud of the past, but anxious for success to be repeated in equal measure in the future.

in Barcelona. Before a big European game many years ago, the by-now retired playmaker penned a provocative article in a local paper on how the visiting team could turn over the Catalonians in the Nou Camp. It prompted fans to go to work and prepare a banner that stretched the length of the pitch. Displayed in full before the game in the stadium, it read 'we hate all traitors here, Alfredo'.

A Bulgarian gives a modern insight into the depth of feeling, animosity and bitterness that divides Spain and exceeds even that felt by supporters of Celtic and Rangers. Barcelona's Hristo Stoichkov reflects on the prospect of ever moving to Madrid: 'No, I am sorry, there is just something about them that winds me up. They say elephants never forget and I guess Bulgarians must be the same. We have got incredibly long memories. How could I possibly play for Madrid after having been public enemy number one there.'

The suggestion of such a move is a 'story fit only for children' to adopt more of the Bulgarian's interesting vernacular, useful in arguing the toss that the Danes are Europe's most mild-mannered beings. The enormously gifted Michael Laudrup actually made the switch from Barça to Real and explained of the 1994 transfer: 'I think nothing of it. Of course, I am conscious of being an ex-Barça player and that rivalry will always exist, but I hope everyone will stop talking of the past. I like to live in the present.' Some hope. Joan Gaspart, Vice President at Barça, responded: 'I wish Laudrup all the luck in the world as a person but all possible disaster with Madrid.' This is passion, the like of which is rarely tasted in Copenhagen.

In fact, most of Spain wish disaster on Madrid. The unpredictable Jesús Gil y Gil, President of city rivals Atlético complains: 'Every day I have to fight against the odds for my club's very existence. The competition in Spain is totally adulterated in favour of Real and Barça. Madrid is a city where 80 per cent of the press is in favour of Real.' Which explains the origins of Gil's nickname amongst the media, 'Caligula'. He would, he confides, rather talk to a horse than a reporter. And, it would appear, also rather than referees. Gil alleged they operate a mafia-style syndicate in support of Real, an outburst in 1995 that earned him an eight-month suspension from the Spanish football authorities.

Blame Franco if you like. They still do in Barcelona. He remains accused of stealing Catalonia of her right to autonomy and banning her language. That the

Michael Laudrup is a rare example of a player who switched from Barcelona to play for Real Madrid, crossing a divide that is much wider than merely the geographical distance between the two great Spanish cities.

bitterness has hit the fortunes of the national side matters not. So long, that is, as Barça finish above Real, the perceived oppressors from the past in the Spanish league.

If rivalry within Spain is ferocious, it is no less intense with neighbours Portugal. So if Real Madrid were the catalyst in establishing the European Cup as a true test of greatness, it is not without irony that Benfica, Portugal's principal glamour side, were instrumental in preventing the competition becoming a footballing forerunner to Rugby League's Wigan-dominated Challenge Cup.

Or rather Eusebio did. The great Johan Cruyff is to the point: 'If you are talking about football in Portugal between 1960 and 1990 then you are talking about Eusebio.' Denis Law adds, as an assessment of the player's true historical worth in a profound sort of way: 'Training may have changed, tactics may have changed but the shape of the ball is still the same. He had tremendous flair and skill and a tremendous shot, but not with his left foot – he didn't use that too much – but his right, superb.'

Perhaps it is because Benfica play in red (Law, after all, is not noted for praising those sporting other colours) but he and Cruyff both perhaps fail to recognise the contribution of the man often pictured alongside Eusebio in photographs of the time wearing a track suit, Bela Guttmann, who steered Benfica to back-to-back Champions Cup wins in 1961 and '62. Indeed, the same could be said of the club directors who declined to pay their shrewd coach a bonus outside the terms of his contract for the second cup win, itself over Madrid by a handsome 5-3 margin in 1962. Eusebio remembers Guttmann, saying to the board that maybe they did not want him to stay. He tested this theory to the full. And left.

Bela Guttmann *(front right, light coloured shirt and tie, with hat in hand)* was as crucial as Eusebio to the success of Benfica in the European Cup, but he ultimately left the club in the belief that he was not adequately rewarded for his coaching contributions. He later returned, but never repeated his early success in winning back-to-back Champions Cups.

Benfica's success in the 1961 European Cup Final against Barcelona 3-2 in Berne broke Real Madrid's stranglehold on the trophy. But it was a fitting succession.

Guttmann, though, acknowledged the brilliance of Eusebio. He is 'gold, gold, gold' said the coach on first sight of the 'barefoot prince of suburban football' who had been plucked from Mafalala in Mozambique in 1961. He even moved the great Coluna, also from the same African country rich in talent, to accommodate his new 'black pearl'. Repayment, maybe, for the loyalty Eusebio showed when arch rivals Sporting Lisbon accused Benfica of poaching him when the inevitable dispute over his signature exploded shortly after his arrival.

Wolstenholme also pays tribute to the brilliance – and sportsmanship – of Eusebio and the genius in handling him shown by Guttmann: 'Eusebio was a great player and a great gentleman. Remember, he was denied a goal by Manchester United's Alex Stepney that would have won the 1968 European Cup Final and he stopped to applaud a great save. I would have felt like killing the keeper. Vinnie Jones probably would have. And Guttmann knew his strengths. Coaches like Guttmann, they had done it all. They would sign a player for what he could do and then let him do it.'

Together Eusebio and Guttmann combined to sustain the European Cup as age and infirmity took their toll on the great Real side. In Wolstenholme's view: 'They picked up the baton. Benfica were a good side. Real had great players but Benfica had Eusebio, a truly great player, as well as many good players. Eusebio

Eusebio, the barefoot prince of suburban football, ball at his feet, was twice denied the European Cup at Wembley, by AC Milan in 1963 *(left)* and Manchester United five years later. Nevertheless, his skills – and brace of goals – were instrumental in the club's 5-3 defeat of Real Madrid in 1962, a result that confirmed Benfica as a great European power of the 1960s.

stood out more than anybody.'

Eusebio himself stands humbly beside the statue outside the Estadio da Luz (the Stadium of Light, a romantic sounding name until you discover Luz is simply a district in Lisbon) which was cast in his name and honours his contribution to the club. He reflects: 'My life is a football. I am not a doctor or a politician, I just love the game.'

His affection served the European Cup well. Although the mighty Madrid had been humbled by Barcelona the previous year well before the final stages of the European Cup, it needed Benfica to give them a good hiding in the 1962 Final for clubs to realise the standards they had set were attainable again. Ones to which all should aspire. Di Stefano admits: 'Like all important games there was a tremendous pressure to win, win, win. We dominated the first half and led at one point 3-2, but the second half was Benfica's.' Spare a thought for Puskas who scored a hat trick and still lost. But his loss was Benfica's and Europe's gain. A competition that could have become a Spanish curiosity was gifted added depth. The destructive monotony of modern-day Wigan in rugby league was avoided.

The trouble, today, with Real Madrid is 'institutional' argues Valdano, a World Cup winner with Argentina and successful in the UEFA Cup with Real as a player before he became the club's manager. The trouble with Benfica is that the club is cursed. Bela Guttmann is making an ungrateful hierarchy pay for not in turn rewarding him.

It is three decades since two of the biggest clubs in Europe won the Champions Cup; Real in 1966 and Benfica four years earlier. Both have featured in Finals, indeed both have fallen at the last hurdle when facing British clubs, the former to Liverpool in 1981 and the latter to Manchester United in 1968. No small drama, too. Remember Stepney again. Eusebio believed he had 'a goal in my boot'. He was denied by the best save of the keeper's entire career.

In Real's case it is not difficult to appreciate what the club's continued failure means to its supporters. Some facts about Benfica help in understanding how serious their drought is in the Portuguese capital. The club has over 100,000 members and more than 20 teams competing under the Benfica banner in different disciplines. Like the Barça motto, Benfica is 'more than a club'. Another

The Estadio da Luz, home to Benfica and fronted by a statue commemorating Eusebio's contribution, both domestic and European, in enhancing the club's rich history.

tangible piece of evidence of the importance of Benfica is provided, inadvertently, by the media. In 1994, when 66 people were killed in a mortar attack on Sarajevo, on the eve of the Benfica–Porto game, page one of the main Lisbon paper covered the atrocity while pages two to six previewed the game, seemingly indifferent to the extent of human carnage. In Lisbon, Benfica are always big news, never more so when they are failing to win the European Cup.

Eusebio's concern at Benfica's inability to win a third European Cup is said to have prompted him to take a rose to the grave of Bela Guttmann in the hope that the offering would end the curse the former coach had placed on his club when refused a bonus to mark his accomplishments.

The evidence of bad spirits? An injury to Coluna during the European Cup Final against AC Milan in 1963 which probably cost Benfica the game, a nut-megged winner conceded through the reliable keeper Costa Pereira's legs in

The European Cup is held aloft by the players of Benfica after the 3-2 defeat of Barcelona in 1961. A second success followed, one year on, but since then the club has failed to lift the trophy again.

defeat against Inter two years later, Stepney's uncanny positioning in 1968. Proof of a curse? Not so. Eusebio, verging on the boastful for perhaps the first time in his career, argues: 'Back in the 1960s, Benfica had good players, young and old. Guttmann was smart. He was coaching Porto and they won the league but he could see that Benfica had the players. People forget that he came back again in 1964 after leaving in 1962 and won nothing in Europe. Benfica will win the European Cup again, but if they don't score they cannot win. That is the case for Benfica today.'

Eusebio, you see, 'believes in Portugal', not talk of curses. And with good reason. Internationally, the country's junior teams have thrived in the early 1990s and many of the same successful youngsters are showing signs of making the transition to full international level. Among them is Joao Pinto, with as many interpretations of his name – plain Joao Pinto, Joao Vieira Pinto, JV Pinto or Joao Pinto II – as he has gifts.

And in Spain? Well, national divisions seem set to plague whoever has the honour of being national team coach, burdened with uniting Royalists and separatists. But a Real side, worthy of wearing the white of Di Stefano and Puskas cannot be far away with young stars like the gifted Raúl emerging.

When Real have a commemorative dinner, the cigars are Montecristo, but a club wrapper rings the luxury leaves covering any trace of Cuban origins. In time, the celebratory smoking will surely honour stars of the future as well as the contributions of the past. Having established a yardstick for European excellence for the generations that followed, it would be a shame if the club's reputation went up in smoke.

be gallant losers in the Final to Real Madrid. Nor were the Hibs players in awe of unfamiliar opponents. They deserved to mix in the company of Di Stefano and Kopa. Four of the memorable 'famous five' of Hibs championship winning side were represented in the 2-0 away and 1-0 home defeats in the semi-final: Smith, Reilly, Turnbull and Ormond. Denied a European Cup success, their enterprise nevertheless deserves, at least to be honoured and acknowledged.

The Munich Air Disaster, the price of Manchester United's adventure into Europe.

Celtic, though, were like United for England, appropriate first Champions Cup winners for Scotland. Glasgow had to wait more than 20 years to be belatedly honoured as the City of Culture, but by the sixties it was already unofficially recognised as home to a healthy eclectic community in addition to a population fundamentally solid with Scottish protestant values. To Parkhead – 'Paradise' – they flocked. It was Celtic, with its origins in the Catholic roots of the city, who were supported by the more enlightened, liberally-minded sections of Glasgow. And although the Catholicism of the city could be as fiercely oppressive as Rome's, with some urban enlightenment came a taste for adventure abroad.

65

The sectarianism of Glasgow also meant Celtic were well prepared for the isolation of foreign jaunts. In some quarters, supporting Celtic is considered tantamount to lining up alongside the Irish Republic, and hence against Scotland and the Union. From this, it is only a small step to suggest that the cause of Irish liberation – achieved by fair means or foul – is also embraced by those who wear the green and white hoops, symbolic perhaps of containment and oppression. The subsequent city rivalry between Celtic and Rangers with its added nationalistic edge is one of the most passionate in world football and can, make Glasgow an unfriendly place for emerald shirts.

And to think that the late Jock Stein, Celtic's greatest manager, and Kenny Dalglish, the club's greatest player were both Protestants. It would disappoint the more zealous followers to learn that the animosity on the fans' side of the pitch perimeter far outstrips that which prevails on the field. John Greig, a 'Ger' with blood as blue as that in the Union Jack, admits: 'Basically we were very friendly. We respected each other because we understood the pressures of being a Celtic or Rangers player.'

For many of the Celtic players who won the European Cup, the whole campaign, appropriately, remembering Busby's words, was in reality something of a busman's holiday, a great experience, a chance to sample different worlds and far-flung places, and diverse populations with which many of them felt greater empathy towards than the Orangemen at home. Indeed, for the personalities of the side – the likes of midfielder Bertie Auld, 'Ten-thirty', and defender Tommy Gemmell, 'Big Tam', for two – it was a chance to make friends and meet people. To sample life.

None sampled it more than Jimmy Johnstone. Diminutive only in stature, Johnstone must have occasionally wondered about the wisdom of continental expeditions so rough was some of the treatment he received from full backs as he danced and jigged down wings all over the continent. But after the game, he would be one of the first to extend a hand. 'Jinky' (by nickname and by nature) was once rested from an international for being, in the opinion of the then management team, not being mentally attuned. In fact, his true crime was the possession of an open mind.

Spirit ran through the side, rich with individuals as diverse as the continent itself. Billy McNeill, 'Caesar' and the captain of the Lisbon Lions (although in truth the game was played in Estoril), who defeated the might of Inter and Herrera to win the coveted trophy, recalls: 'We did everything well, worked hard and played hard. It was all part of being in the team. We had some real characters. It was like the old Labour Party, diverse views all working together for a common goal.'

Jock Stein, Celtic manager, and as much a father-figure to the club as Busby was to United, had sensed the side was 'going somewhere' after a Scottish Cup win in 1965. The league followed a year later and before the team knew it they were indeed on the move, to the continent; to Switzerland, France, the old Yugoslavia, and Czechoslovakia, before Portugal and the final hurdle, Internazionale and the 1967 European Cup Final. Travel, though, held no fear for the Scots. An intrepid following of fans trailed them. One such traveller, legend has it, memorably (or should it be forgetfully) drove to the Med only to return by plane swept up in the 'emotion' of the affair, leaving his car abandoned.

Truly a holiday spirit. And therein was the key to Celtic's success, according to their captain. But what by now had become, by reaching the Final, at least a mildly stressful foray on behalf of the Catholic sections of the Scottish nation, was defused by Stein who, like all great managers, masterfully relaxed his players with agreeable distractions.

Nothing, though, to blunt the performance. McNeill remembers: 'The night before the game against Inter, England were playing and it was on television. There was a Scots lad that Jock knew who had set himself up out in Portugal. I remember going to watch the game at his place. We walked back through some woods and it was so casual. It helped relax us. We'd already done the preparation and been told to stay out of the sun. We knew we were there to do a job and that it was not a holiday, but we were very relaxed.'

Stein's psychological plan continued right up to the game, including pro-active methods against the enemy. Herrera had sent out some subs to claim a bench alongside the pitch from which to watch the game, but the big man, ably assisted by his own replacements and support team, promptly shoved the holding party off Celtic's chosen pew leaving them to sit in seats less favoured by Inter's famous emperor. Stein was acting on the advice of Liverpool's Bill Shankly, the only English-based manager in the stadium still pricked from Liverpool's defeat by Inter in the semi-finals in 1965. Shankly, one presumes, suspected Herrera of crimes more serious than life and death.

And in the dressing-room? Bertie Auld, as ever the master of ceremonies, recalls: 'I remember Jock's speech before we went out into this long, long tunnel. He said, I'm proud of you, you've made history getting here, go out and play the way you can.' Inspired – for the players were very much in awe of Stein – Auld and his team-mates joined Inter in the shade under the grandstand. At that moment it seemed appropriate for Auld to sing. He did, and everyone joined in, all the Celtic songs: 'If you know your history, it's enough to make your heart go, ooooaaaaaaah' was the sound. 'We should have been wearing kilts instead of fitba pants' says Auld.

But when Inter scored a penalty after seven minutes it was if as the Scots had been sent home to think again. Using the Wolstenholme scale for converting Italian goals into a general European score, 1-0 down to Inter was equivalent to 3-0 against normal opposition. Game over.

Left back Tommy Gemmell disagreed. 'It was the best thing that ever happened to us,' he argues. 'As Italians they were very defensive minded [and set out to protect the lead] and there wasn't a team in the world who could play against us like that and not lose matches.'

Gemmell himself could do no more than score to prove his point. He duly did, after 63 minutes, although not without a moment's reflection as he swept a shot into the net from outside the box: 'If the move had broken down and Inter had gone and scored I'd have had my backside kicked. Jim Craig [the right back] had overlapped on the right [and squared the ball to Gemmell who scored]. I'd have got a bollocking because I shouldn't have been up there with Jim.'

It was, though, one of those nights. If Gemmell should have stayed back, then both Celtic players clearly in offside positions should have been elsewhere. Neither, in truth, should keeper Bobby Simpson have earlier found himself well out of his box with the ball at his feet and Inter forwards bearing down on him at great pace. Unless, that is, the linesman could be relied upon to overlook the brace of offenders (he did) and Simpson could be relied upon to backheel the ball to Clark (he could).

The latter manoeuvre was perhaps a turning point in the match. Simpson's train of thought was inspired: 'The ball came down the park so I ran out. I was going to blooter it as there was no one about. Then an Inter boy ran across and I realised that if I kicked it it would hit him and go towards the goal and I'd be beaten for pace. So I backheeled it.'

It still worries Simpson: 'I often lie in bed at night and think what would have happened if it had gone wrong. I think I might have been lynched.'

McNeill reckons he would have been all right: 'The final score was 2-1 but we should have won by four or five. It was only the brilliance of their keeper Sarti who kept them in the game. We thought he might have been the weak link.'

But the true weakness of Estoril was more fundamental, and recurring: Scottish exuberance. After the final whistle had gone, Chalmers' strike, and Celtic's second, having proved decisive, the ground become the venue for merriment that strayed into mischief. McNeill remembers: 'I was left on my own after the final whistle. By the time I got back to the dressing-room I had lost the Inter shirt

The pleadings of Inter's goal-keeper, Sarti, for an offside decision against 'Big Iam' Gemmell's equaliser for Celtic in the 1967 European Cup Final in Estoril were ignored. The Scottish champions went on to lift the trophy with a 2-1 victory.

Bobby Simpson gathers a cross against Inter in the 1967 European Cup Final. The keeper had to resort to a less safe backheel in possession outside his area in the same game, but his coolness under pressure inspired his team-mates to success.

I had swapped, and my boots. After the game on the bus we passed a car and they were waving socks and boots at us. But they were unimportant really.' Most certainly when you consider that Simpson, for all his backheeling exploits could hardly smile. His false teeth remained forgotten in the back of one of the nets.

For all the differences and divisions between Celtic and Rangers fans, they share the same reckless tendency to over-celebrate. Five years on from Estoril, similar scenes, but with more menace, blighted Spain when Rangers beat Dynamo Moscow 3-2 to win the Cup Winners' Cup in Barcelona. Success at the Nou Camp was greeted with a pitch invasion that provoked a baton charge – a taste of things to come for British fans in Europe. The presentation of the cup took place in a room under the stands.

John Greig, Rangers and Scotland hard man, laments: 'It was a bit of an anti-climax. By the time I got to the dressing-room, the team were all in the bath. I don't think half the Rangers fans ever saw that cup.'

For Scots abroad, cups often seem to be to drink from, not to parade.

Spirits, in contrast, haunted Manchester United's pursuit of European fulfilment. The club's players abroad carried a much heavier responsibility than Celtic's best the stars of any British club for that matter. Following Munich, winning the European Cup became a crusade. The air disaster, which claimed, among others, the life of Duncan Edwards (who, had he lived, might well have kept centurion Bobby Moore's haul of England caps down to a less historic tally), imposed a heavy burden to complete the journey and win the very trophy the Babes had sought. Mercifully, for the memory of those others who perished on that return flight from Champions Cup quarter final success against Red Star Belgrade – Byrne, Pegg, Taylor, Colman, Jones, Whelan and Bent, as well as Edwards along with respected scribes – they did, winning the European Cup ten years later in 1968, at Wembley. With hindsight, it is little surprise the club stumbled thereafter.

Manchester United finally accomplished what those before had set out to achieve the year after Celtic. But it was not with the team Busby would have chosen to accomplish the feat. Bobby Charlton, whom Busby would most certainly have nominated to be present on any occasion Manchester United won a trophy muses on the success: 'Every dream he ever had came true that night,

(*Below left*) Willie Johnston rises to score his first and Rangers' second in their 3-2 defeat of Dynamo Moscow in the 1972 European Cup Winners' Cup Final in Barcelona. (*Below right*) Captain John Greig clutches the spoils Outside, fans were exhibiting a tendency to over celebrate that has blighted Scottish achievement in Europe more than once.

maybe not with the players he would have wanted, but certainly on the day.'

To some extent, it was impossible for the Munich survivors to think other-wise. Bill Foulkes, whose career embraced the club's every foray into Europe until he retired confided years later: 'I had something else to play for, those who died in the crash. I had a responsibility. I felt that. They were friends of mine. I'll never forget their faces. I see them every day, they are still clear.'

Charlton who was thrown clear from the wreckage to safety added, years on: 'I don't think about the accident, but the people involved. Those that were killed were great friends of mine. I have just been lucky. It is unbelievable really that all your pals are killed and you hardly have a scratch. Sometimes it doesn't seem right. Their memory will always be at Manchester United.'

In truth United's pursuit of the trophy in 1968 reached a gripping peak in the semi-final against, appropriately, Real Madrid. Then, like Gemmell's unexpected appearance just outside Inter's penalty box for Celtic in Portugal, it was another defender, Foulkes, who was to intervene decisively, inspired by Busby. After a 1-0 first leg win at Old Trafford, United found themselves 3-1 down at half time in the Bernabeu and mentally broken. Busby himself, well shaken by the reversals, reminded them all, 'You are only one goal down.' The players were revived.

Shortly after the restart Sadler cancelled out the aggregate deficit. United were level. Later, the ball at Best's feet, the call came for a most unlikely hero's greatest moment. Charlton maintains he had never seen Foulkes leave his own half during all the time they had played together. Indeed Nobby Stiles shouted at him to stay back as he made his way forward. Foulkes jokes that he was quickly out of the short-sighted Stiles' view: 'I was in the box to see if George would cross it and there was nobody else. George looked up and had a second look as though he couldn't believe it.' From the cross, the centre half slotted the ball home with ease. Matt Busby's only mistake as a manager? Never playing Bill Foulkes at centre forward.

On the comeback that ensured the Wembley Final, Charlton concludes: 'In the second half, Real lost it. We probably kidded ourselves into thinking that they could play like that for 90 minutes. And, to be fair, they didn't usually play against a side like us. We were coming at them all the time even though we were behind.'

After that, a second high was perhaps expecting too much. The game itself

Manchester United's centre half Bill Foulkes chose well the only moment of his career to leave his defensive post. He levelled the scores in the club's semi-final second leg 3-3 draw with Real Madrid to secure on aggregate a place in the Final at Wembley in 1968.

that clinched the trophy, against Benfica, at Wembley, May 1968 was no classic. The 4-1 score line after extra time flattered United, although they did have a goal disallowed. Wolstenholme, commentating to the nation, spoke directly to Best after he scored, deliberately ignoring the referee's whistle in an effort to

George Best scores Manchester United's second goal against Benfica at Wembley in extra time in the 1968 European Cup Final. Brian Kidd added a third and Bobby Charlton a fourth (and his second) to complete a 4-1 success.

raise the element of excitement: 'It's no goal Georgie. I've got a feeling he knew it wasn't, but it is all good practice.' Also at the microphone was former England manager Walter Winterbottom whose precise analysis midway through the game best summed it up: 'United are playing with great heart and vigour. They want to be just a little bit more careful with their finishing.'

At least in the end they were. Best's crucial tie breaker in extra time ended the 1-1 full time deadlock and ushered in a further two strikes, a second for Charlton who had scored the opener in normal time and one for Brian Kidd, on his nineteenth birthday. Wolstenholme almost rushed George into burying the ball into the Wembley net after he had gained possession with only one man to beat: 'Best, he's got a great chance, he must score, he has.' George, meanwhile, had his thoughts fixed on something completely different: 'I'd made up my mind that I would take it to the line and head it in but the keeper got up quickly so I just knocked it in.'

For such a team, extra time, even against the mighty Benfica in the Final on an energy-sapping night, held no fears, although Charlton admits: 'The trophy was very heavy. We were very tired.' Hardly surprising. It was the end of a decade's quest.

Within six years of winning the European Cup Manchester United were relegated. A year earlier, Best left Old Trafford, having announced his retirement from the game. Although he played again, it was for clubs other than United, and many of them were unworthy.

Best went from bad to worse. The start of United's decline preceded his and was more understandable. The sustained pursuit of the European Cup – and the

David Sadler wears the object of Matt Busby's ten-year continental quest, the European Cup. George Best, in a white Benfica shirt to his right, thought the victory would be the first of many. He was wrong.

75

belief that many of the players who years before began the long journey that culminated with Wembley deserved more than just to travel hopefully — meant rebuilding the side with the next decade's domestic goals in mind had been postponed. After 1968, too. In some ways it would have been disrespectful to dismantle the team. Illogical too while Europe remained the goal. For this, experience was paramount.

For all these reasons, no one even considered the retirement of the manager. Great players like Denis Law remained in awe of Busby right up to his death in 1994. He was, in some respects, irreplaceable in the eyes of many of the players. In Law's case, the day he knocked on Busby's door to ask for a pay rise, he did not need to open it to leave. Men of greater stature than the flamboyant self-confident Scot had been similarly cut down to size. By doing so Busby earned their respect.

Best, too, was eventually broken, although Busby would have been the last to oversee such destruction and few at the time could have predicted the Belfast boy's demise. Best's future was perhaps too full of personal dissatisfaction for anyone to save him. Best even felt dissatisfied with his personal performance against Benfica. On an earlier occasion in 1965 when the teams met in the Estadio da Luz, United had thrashed the home side 5-1 and the nickname El Beatle was born. But Wembley 1968 was no better than average by comparison: 'I began to pick out a few things that I did well which for me told me I didn't have a great game.'

The effect of the game though, on Best, was immense. Charlton said of his former colleague that he had got it all 'a little bit too soon'. Best concurs, sort of: 'I felt after we won the Cup in 1968 everyone was saying that's it, we have done it. I was 22. I wasn't going to reach my peak for seven or eight years and I listened to everyone saying that we've achieved what we wanted to achieve, what we set out to achieve and it seemed as if they were talking as if it was all over. I was only starting. I thought they should have been saying that it was the first of many.'

In truth, the goal, the obsession founded in the cruel denial of Munich, had been all-consuming. The club's long-term future — once the immediate repercussions of the disaster had been resolved — was put on hold while the pursuit of a

Best and the ball, inseparable companions at Manchester United until the club lost its desire for success.

more immediate justice, denied the Babes, became all-important. Once achieved, Busby, then aged 59, remained but without the same purpose. The managers who subsequently attempted to replace him were, according to Best, only managers in the loosest sense of the word. None could motivate him, and the last – Tommy Docherty – was, he maintained, 'a bullshitter'.

Best was disappointed. He believes the club slumped after its greatest hour through its failure to build again: 'When those wonderful players I had been brought up with – Charlton, Law, Crerand, Stiles – went into decline, United made no real effort to buy the best replacements available. I was left struggling among fellas who should not have been allowed through the door at Old Trafford. I was doing it on my own and I was just a kid. It sickened me to the heart that we ended up just about the worst team in the First Division.'

After Wembley 1968, United had the task of replacing those who represented the spirit of Munich. Sadly, they learned that you can't replace the irreplaceable.

Best, subsequently European Footballer of the Year, retired around five years later, having been already driven out of Old Trafford by people he claimed had told lies. Such a capacity is beyond bare statistics. Alex Ferguson, the first manager to come close to filling Busby's void, supplies some pertinent facts about Best: 'Look at George's scoring record, 137 goals in 361 league games, a total of 179 for United in 466 matches played. That's phenomenal for a man who did not get his fair share of gift goals that come to specialist strikers, who nearly always had to beat a man to score. At Old Trafford, they reckoned Bestie had double jointed ankles.'

Fame, infamy? It is all relative. An often repeated anecdote springs to mind. Best is in a fabulous New York hotel with one of the Miss Worlds who indulged him, and thousands of dollars won at the casino on the bed, when a bellboy, from Belfast and therefore a long standing admirer, knocks on the door with the ordered iced champagne. As George stuffs a large bill in his pocket as a tip, he is asked, with great sincerity, 'Where did it all go wrong?'

As individuals, the heroes of Celtic's finest hour have had mixed experiences since their own achievements set the European agenda for Rangers; in management – Billy McNeill failed in Stein's chair – as pundits and in other fields. Of the starting eleven, four subsequently ran pubs, one became a dentist, another a fireman, one drove a lorry and one sold insurance. Reunions are regular. It seems doubtful if those in attendance in 1995 knew what stone correctly commemorates weddings that have also survived relatively unscathed for 28 years. Perhaps the wives in marriages beginning in 1967 who remain with their husbands deserve green emeralds each year.

And George? After a spell in prison – Pentonville Number 76215 – numerous brushes with the law subsequently, alcoholic outbursts and of course *Wogan*, there is more than a sporting chance that people will still remember with fondness the boy who crossed the Irish Sea, and, encouraged by an older pioneer in Busby, conquered a continent.

The second best story about George – and probably less apocryphal – after the hotel in New York is the one where he is watching a penalty shoot out on television and it comes down to the final take. A wag asks: 'Who would like to be in his shoes then?' himself personally frightened at the prospect. 'I would,' mutters George, over and over again, more to himself than anyone present, 'I would.'

If Manchester United were the fathers of England in Europe, George was the errant son, who, although happy to spot the ball, had to contend with the fact that the ultimate triumph took its toll on the family.

Whatever happened to *Wogan*?

HOLLAND

STRICTLY
BUSINESS

Johan Cruyff of Ajax shoots against Juventus in the 1973
European Cup Final on the way to a 1-0 win, a success that
confirmed the Dutch as masters in the art of nurturing talent.

It was clear very early in the life of Ronaldo that the boy from Bento Ribeiro was born to wear the world famous gold shirt of his country. It was his destiny. Gifted with a name rich in the traditional Samba mix of vowels and consonants – a resonant enough combination to satisfy any excitable South American commentator – it was just a question of when. Alfonsinho, Augustino, Rivelino, Carlos Alberto, Pele, Ronaldo, BRAZIL! So natural. The continuation of a tradition. The beautiful game goes on, and on, and on.

Ronaldo: flair by name, flair by nature. Enough, indeed, to persuade PSV Eindhoven to pay around £4 million in the transfer market for one of the world's most exciting teenagers when he was still too young to vote. Flair in abundance. The name, most definitely, said it all. It was already abbreviated from his parents' choice – Ronaldo Luiz Nazario de Lima. Such details matter when you remember that all great Brazilians adopt shortened versions of their names for greater empathy with their admirers.

The good people of Eindhoven, too, would embrace their latest talented import. How romantic that the Dutch had been seduced by a South American tradition.

An expensive affair? On the face of it, too much money simply to indulge in a fantasy. And so it was. The reality of Ronaldo's arrival was rather less starry-eyed. The logic of the transfer was hardly founded on fanciful 1970 World Cup nostalgia alive in an Eindhoven boardroom. It was more rooted in the disciplined business acumen that runs right through the Philips dominated club. Buying Ronaldo was good business. Or so it would prove to be in time.

Such is the way at PSV, and indeed, at Ajax and Feyenoord, together, the three giants of Dutch football. After all, before Ronaldo, there had been Romario who thrilled thousands of fans at the Philips Stadium before moving to Barcelona. PSV cleared a healthy profit on the sale of Romario. In time, they expect to do a similar deal with his fellow countryman Ronaldo. It will be the same with their home-grown talent when the time comes for them to be cashed in. There will be plenty of buyers.

To some extent, PSV – unusually for such sharp operators – had already been beaten to the punch with Ronaldo. Jairzinho, a fellow countryman, who made his mark among many memorable Brazilian imprints on the 1970 World Cup, had

Ronaldo of PSV Eindhoven, bought for £4 million from Brazil, an investment for the club that will, along with others also being carefully nurtured, ultimately yield a healthy profit.

taken the precaution of overseeing the purchase of a 50 per cent interest in the then 15-year-old through Promocões Furacão (a company of which Jairzinho owned half), even though top Brazilian club Flamengo declined to offer Ronaldo a contract. Jairzinho's foresight – and Flamengo's error – became apparent only when PSV sat down with Ronaldo's eventual club, Cruzeiro de Belo Horizonte, to negotiate a fee. £4 million was considerably more than they expected to pay.

It mattered not. PSV doubted they would be made to look slow so easily next time. And even allowing for an inflated agent's fee, it was still a good deal. And Dutch football has never been able to turn down a good deal, even when a Mr Ten Per Cent, like Jairzinho, takes a slice. Most often it is the 'family silver' that's for sale, the home-grown talent. In this case, the club moved swiftly to deal in Brazilian futures. Whatever the nationality, at PSV it is all human currency. Football in Holland is a trade.

If investors could buy shares in Dutch football, PEPS, Granny Bonds, even National Savings Accounts and the most secure building societies would cease to be the safest of homes for the ultra cautious speculators' money. The basis of this commercial success is different to the skilled off-the-field exploitation of Manchester United. Britain's most popular club has merely had to establish exactly how big the market is, and then supply it to achieve blue chip status. Dutch football has had to nurture its own product – players – market it, by competing with the rival European outlets which they ultimately hope to enhance with their own goods, and then replace offloaded stock to keep competing at a level that maintains the profile enjoyed at the beginning of the cycle. The mass production of footballers. Perhaps, with this process in mind, it is of little surprise that Philips, the multi-national electronics conglomerate, chose to form a close partnership with PSV to the extent that board members of the club also occupy influential positions within the European arm of the company. Both are, after all, in the business of producing and selling parts.

Philips technology may be complex, but for PSV the process of producing footballers is simple, the purchase of the odd Brazilian teenager aside. Select and train your own from the local catchment area, win a European trophy with them – or at least perform well on the European stage – cash in the asset by selling it abroad and reinvest in the youth programme to keep the conveyor belt of replacements coming to ensure there is no dip in performance. The last aspect is important. The Dutch public enjoy their football but without tolerating sub-standard quality. Failure quickly results in falling attendances and consequently a reduced turnover, the beginnings of a vicious circle. It is the tightrope that the three big clubs – for they, in truth, are Dutch football – PSV, Feyenoord and of course, Ajax, walk. Playing standards must be maintained or crowds – and income –

could dwindle. Then the need to sell could exceed the capacity to replenish.

The achievements of these clubs to date suggest the balance has been about right for some time. For five years, between 1969 and 1973, there was a Dutch club in the European Cup Final, a run that yielded four trophies, three in a row for Ajax and one for Feyenoord. PSV have also won the European Cup, in 1988. Having a trio of clubs with Champions Cup wins against their names has proved beyond the Spanish, German and Portuguese leagues, well beyond the French, too. There has been further success as well, periodically in the UEFA Cup and occasionally in the Cup Winners' Cup. And, of course, Ajax beat Milan 1-0 in 1995 to become Champions of Europe once again.

The national team, too, has maintained this level of achievement. Their record since 1974, of two World Cup Final appearances and a European Championships success in Germany in 1988, is stong currency. In the latter conflict (if it involves Germany, to the Dutch it always becomes a conflict) the home nation were defeated by the Dutch who went on to win the tournament. This, and other Dutch conquests, either in the national orange or by those wearing the domestic colours of PSV, Ajax and Feyenoord, are all the more remarkable when you consider that Dutch football was amateur until 1954 when semi-professional status for some was sanctioned. Full blown professionalism albeit only for the league's top stars came ten years later.

The Ajax team which dominated the European Cup at the beginning of the seventies provided the core of Holland's enchanting international side of the same period *(below)* including Cruyff, Neeskens, Krol, Haan, Rep and Suurbier.

Dutch football, though, has never been simply a financial whirl for the players, although many have left in search of wealth. Style dominates. Totally. Indeed, 'total football' was the phrase coined in the early 1970s to describe the Dutch style. A system in which players were able to adopt any position and fill any role within a team's strategy. The whirl. How it thrilled the world, dizzy with admiration. An orange blur.

It was wholly appropriate that this popular style evolved in Holland. Free-thinking is encouraged in Dutch schools and within religious organisations to a degree that would appal staunch disciplinarians of English public school extraction. Frowns, too, from the pulpit. Dutch protestants have a more open-minded attitude to spiritual matters than their Anglican cousins abroad. This broad church is reflected in their football. There is never a Sunday-school mentality to the overlapping full back. In England, such defensive frivolity is a sin. Not so in the religion of Dutch football.

Of course, Dutch football has some disciplines. Of course there are positions, tactics, and winning is important. But all in good time. Such patience means the players, on reaching footballing maturity, have versatility greatly exceeding that possessed by the already pigeon-holed English teenager. In Holland all outfield players can cover for a colleague when he is temporarily absent from the field of play, or permanently indisposed in the treatment room. Rounded citizens; total footballers.

Total football is one thing, anarchy another. The freedom of thought that evolves in a carefree, previously part-time, world has a sting. In Holland the unrestricted development of players always seems to manifest itself ultimately in disharmony within the squads of even the most successful teams. The source of Dutch football's greatest strength is also the source of its worst feature. Johan Cruyff, the greatest Dutch player of all time, acknowledges: 'We Dutchmen are pig-headed.' Indeed they are.

Bobby Robson, who managed PSV for two years between 1990 and 1992, winning back-to-back championships, explained to one player whom he had substituted that he would understand the motivation behind his withdrawal only when the player himself became a manager. The individual will not have taken kindly to being patronised.

Bobby Robson managed PSV for two years and, like his predecessors, had to accept that the club would not risk breaking the bank on a gamble in the way that Mediterranean clubs have in the past, and will continue to in the future.

Robson, who, of course, steered England to World Cup quarter and semi-finals, winces at the thought of coping with Dutch national rebellions. He recalls the difficulties Dutch coaches encounter when 'the baby rears its ugly head' having always been encouraged to say his bit at a young age. 'The players have tried to say who should run the national team,' Robson relates, aghast at the very idea that dissenters, led by Ruud Gullit (maybe the second best Dutch player of all-time), argued for the replacement of Dick Advocaat before the 1994 World Cup. 'Gullit was like a spoiled child before the last World Cup. He said he didn't like the coach so he would not play. Unfortunately, this side of Dutch football has been there for everyone to see. The players become too powerful.'

For Robson, a frightening thought. Lunatics taking over the asylum? No, Robson's fear is that the system he favours, the tight close knit squad that British coaches cultivate, would break down. Indeed it would. But Dutch football continues to thrive. Why? Because disruptive outpourings do not disturb the continuation of the business cycle. In fact, dissent is the very oil that lubricates and ensures its smooth running. After all, it is easier to justify offloading the more disruptive. And, happily for the PSV board, and the Ajax decision-makers, the most argumentative – none more so than Cruyff and Gullit – are usually the most gifted. There is good money to be made in dissent. It is easier to sell an angry player than encourage him to sign a new contract.

And so the wheels of the Dutch machine turn. And, like the best corporations there is no sentiment. They will sell anyone. The Agnellis will dip into Fiat's glove compartment for money to sustain their precious Juventus; Berlusconi will commit the yield of television commercials from his channels to refurbishing his beloved AC Milan; but Philips will not so much as change a light bulb, above and beyond the company's contractual commitment to the club, agreed at the beginning of the year. PSV, of course, want to win. Most definitely against Ajax and Feyenoord. In Europe, too. They have had a taste of what that was like and the taste was very sweet. The fans demand it, albeit less ferociously than they do in European football's heartlands – Italy, Spain, England, Scotland. But goals will not be pursued with the recklessness that regularly features elsewhere. The Dutch emotional about football? Never (although against Germany they have had their moments).

Robson accepted the close relationship that exists between Philips and PSV, based on balancing both sets of books. Of his two years in charge at PSV, he recalls: 'Philips give an injection at the beginning of the season and that is it. There is a marketing department and commercial department and their job is to bring in money from outside sources to back up gate receipts so the club can compete in the transfer market to some extent. But I don't think the general manager of the club, if he went to the board and said we need to buy players, would get the cash. They give the [pre-season] money and it is substantial and that is it. PSV want success and try for it, but they would not break the club on a gamble. Real would, Barcelona would, Milan would. They would all move heaven and earth to get a player, but PSV are not like that. Neither are Feyenoord and Ajax. They are all selling clubs because they know they have replacements on the way. They try to get the best possible team for the least money.'

For a man like Robson, so gripped by football, such cold commercialism must have been depressing. It is, though, difficult to argue against the logic and, most importantly, the results. Ajax were founded in 1900 by – one assumes free-thinking – businessmen who used to meet on Sundays, sporting the day's preferred dress – morning coat and topper – and talk football. Today they would salute the evolution into corporate football of their original Sabbath industry. Hats off, as well, to PSV. A ripple of applause, too, from the Philips boardroom. Their reasoning? Sell your camcorder for more than it cost you to make it and produce another one just as good to use yourself. For camcorders, read footballers. Except the money is better. Good business indeed.

Total football. Today, you might think that it is yet another sponsorship deal; a petroleum company adding its financial clout to that of the existing patrons whose cash already fuels the world game's escalating salaries and transfer fees. In the 1970s the game was relatively commercial free. The only confusion relating to total football was in the havoc it created in the defences of the tactically and technically limited. Total havoc.

Comparable devastation is frequently found in the nurseries of mainland Europe. There, young minds are allowed to roam free and develop natural gifts within a larger framework of parental control. Looser than most English schools allow for sure. The end result should be, hopefully, individuals who have had the chance to establish talents for which they possess natural gifts. This way, if the peg is round, it has a better chance of ending up in a round hole.

So in Holland. So also with Dutch football. In coaching the game, the nursery equivalent is a playing field, the children eight years and upwards, and the toy a football; the best ever invented. The big clubs of Rotterdam (Feyenoord), Amsterdam (Ajax) and Eindhoven (PSV) host training sessions *en masse* for the local schools who do not involve themselves with the sport. Most important to the process is its liberty. Individual gifts are allowed to flourish. By the time the young protégés reach double figures in years, the three clubs have a core of talented children with minds uncluttered with tactics. Physical changes follow, as nature dictates, but the formative years have been seized to ensure that the clumsiness of puberty is merely a temporary suspension of ball control.

The end products are footballers who together can function as a glorious, interchangeable unit. Bobby Robson purrs when he thinks of the combination of such gifts that was the Ajax 1995 Champions Cup winning team: 'They make ten passes and are not worried about getting anywhere because they know they will eventually. The goalie rolls it to the full back who plays it across the back who lays

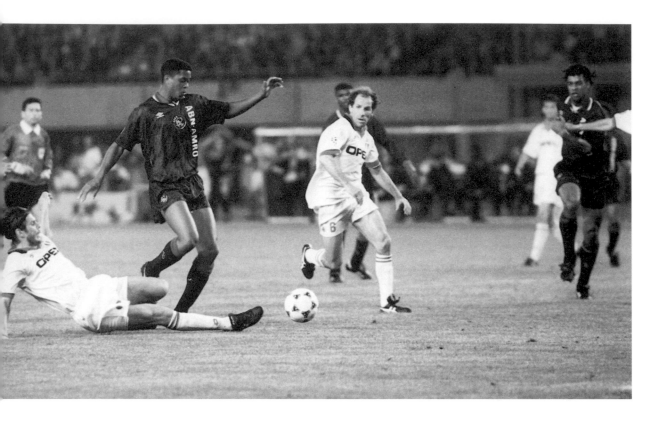

Patrick Kluivert's goal in the 1995 European Cup Final against AC Milan restored his club Ajax as champions of Europe for the first time in more than 20 years. The success was founded in the club's extraordinarily successful youth policy. On the night, Kluivert was still only 18.

it off to the winger on the overlap and finishes off the move. They all handle the ball well. In England we give it to the full back and what does he do with it? He gets rid of it up the field. He cannot put it inside and get it back, put it back inside, play a one-two...'

At Ajax the process of producing a European Cup winning side begins with its annual open day when around 1500 children are invited from the local area. From this batch are chosen about forty talents, the majority of whom are expected ultimately to make up future Champions League competitors.

At PSV, Robson remembers from his two years as Director of Coaching: 'Feyenoord, PSV, Ajax, they all tackle it the same way. The children come in at around eight years old and are put into the bottom age band, 8 to 10, with 10 to 12, 12 to 14 above them. PSV ran about thirteen teams when I was there. There is no schoolboy football, it is all arranged by the clubs. They stage tournaments for the young players to play in but it is kind of non-competitive, never on a full sized pitch.'

Goalless to start with, too. Arnold Muhren related as much to Robson when the former played in midfield for Ipswich under the stewardship of the latter. Robson recalls: 'Arnold had every pass in the book, 5 yards, 50 yards. I said to him, how did he learn his skills, and he said it was because every day in training as a young boy he would play eight-a-side, with ball possession the aim, and count the number of times they could play pass and move, with swerves and dummies. Then the coach might finally say, let's put the goals up now.'

Robson demonstrates. Remember, he played for England in two World Cups. But he cannot quite master the drag back with which Muhren thrilled. Maybe it's the carpet. Maybe, at over 60, Robson is no Stanley Matthews. It is certainly not for want of trying on his part.

Back to the future. Robson rejects the notion that the excellent technique of the Dutch is inborn – which begs the question, why not in Britain? In Holland they believe that all skill is taught, by taking advantage of impressionable years. 'The Dutch children are not more gifted, inherently,' maintains Robson on his first-hand experiences. And England's lament? 'They just get them early, at eight. In England during my Ipswich days, we couldn't get players before they were 14.' Too late: 'Concert pianists are introduced to the piano at five or six years and end up performing at 13.'

'I used to see training at PSV with the youngsters and it was all with the ball, dribble, pass, little turns, headers, on small pitches with small goals, four-a-side. They would develop the players all round, get them to go forward, back. They would not play in set positions until 13 at the earliest. In England, the coaching is done by teachers and it is all about playing in matches for the under nines and under tens. It isn't about training. It was about teachers wanting their teams to win. You must win and you must play to your position. You can hear the teachers shouting from the touch line. Competitive football comes too early in Britain.'

The coaches in Holland stand silently, observing. They know what to look for, too. The majority are former players, some full internationals in their day. All are respected and most importantly, their work is valued. For the Dutch, it is a question of priorities. In Britain, only banks cultivate the young so intensely. In Holland the coaches are the ones saying yes.

Johan Cruyff, the master, took his youthful experience at Ajax to Barcelona both as a player and subsequently as a manager. As a result the players in Catalonia are encouraged as they mature to work on inherent weaknesses; a right handed/footed player will be schooled in heading left to right, a direction that will be less natural. The training prepares him for an attack when the cross is delivered from the left and so on.

Meanwhile, in Holland, the coaches themselves are granted the time and stable environment the players enjoy to develop their own capabilities. The stability complements the continuity. Once again we turn to the example of Ajax, fresh from European Cup success. Who knows if they would have lifted the trophy without the sympathetic handling of their mentor, Louis Van Gaal, who rose from youth to senior coach along with the very players who won the trophy.

Those who benefit from the schooling of coaches have been chosen early. Cruyff argues, depressingly for those twenty- and thirty-somethings who still indulge in dreams at the local park on Sunday mornings, that the time to decide on young footballers is the age of 12: 'At that age you know whether or not a boy is going to be a player. There are fundamental skills which you have or don't have, which cannot be taught after that age.' Like the Cruyff turn.

With some Dutch sides, it was a surprise indeed that the eleven who emerged from the dressing-room sported the same shirts. There is no Bob Hoskins equivalent in Holland because Dutch footballers already like to talk; to the coach, the managing director, the newspapers, in fact anyone who cares to listen. To keep the cackle manageable and to focus the energy of the inherently gifted proved beyond most browbeaten coaches in the 1950s and early 1960s. And this before money took a grip on the game.

Inevitably, though, when a strong enough man arrived and after the transition from uncaring amateurs to hard-nosed professionals had been completed, success followed. Enter Rinus Michels, a no-nonsense coach who was invited by Ajax in 1964 to mould together the sum of the part to see if the whole could, in this case, be even greater.

Don't mess with Rinus Michels. The players didn't. They were too tired to argue. Piet Keizer, a classically Dutch temperamental winger and the antithesis of the coach – but whose best years as an Ajax player coincided with Michels' reign

Rinus Michels, who coached Ajax to three European Cup triumphs, from 1971 to 1973, was a tough disciplinarian whose attitude to those who did not agree with his methods – and being in Holland, there were a few – was simply to let them leave.

– remembers: 'When Michels took over he changed the playing staff considerably. And he changed the training schedule even more. His was the hardest physical preparation I ever had. We sometimes had four sessions a day. He also introduced the Italian system of taking players away for a period of concentrated training before a big match. We would start in the morning and carry on until the evening. Michels was by no means a miserable man, but he was very strict with the players and there were a lot of arguments about discipline. The message was pretty clear. Those who did not like it would have to leave.'

Some did. But not before the team had appeared in four European Cup Finals – losing to AC Milan 4-1 in 1969 but winning three in a row from 1971 to 1973, defeating both Panathinaikos and Inter 2-0 and Juventus by a single goal. A great team indeed. Complete. And deserving of the title the Best in Europe. In their final successful campaign in 1973 they defeated Real Madrid both home (2-1) and away (1-0) en route to success against Juventus in the Final. Real may no longer have boasted the gifted Di Stefano. Nevertheless, the Dutch supremacy over the old European Kings was appropriately symbolic.

Ajax secured their first European Cup at Wembley against Panathinaikos in 1971 with goals from Van Dijk *(above left)* and Haan. It would be three years before another team would celebrate a winning strike in the Champions Cup Final.

If Ajax were the new Real, Cruyff was the new Di Stefano; an equally effective fulcrum for his team. Before the advent of Premiership squad numbers, Cruyff's international number 14 was a symbol of excellence. A team player, a leader, a goalscorer and a creator, Cruyff should have retired the shirt when he quit the game, after having journeyed to Spain and America, before returning cheekily to play for Ajax's arch rivals Feyenoord (think of Eric Cantona moving from Leeds to Manchester United) just to prove he had not mellowed.

For Ajax, the end of an era came when the arguments began, and Cruyff was as vociferous as he was gifted. Inevitably the big money offer came, nearly £1 million, in 1973 – a huge sum. Inevitably he left. His departure to Barcelona signalled the end of the great Ajax days. In truth he was, by this time, simply too big for Dutch football – and so the rest of the team followed, Neeskens also to Barcelona, Rep to Valencia in Spain and Haan to Anderlecht in Belgium.

Ajax could have equalled or even surpassed Real Madrid's record of five consecutive Champions Cups. Gerrie Muhren, older brother of gifted Arnold, and himself a rare talent who played his part in the treble of cup wins before leaving, believes: 'We could have won the European Cup another three or four times if we had stayed together. But there were jealousies and tensions.'

The emotions fuelled the beginings of the Dutch football exporting machine. Ajax were eliminated in round two – after a bye – of their third European Cup defence in 1974 by CSKA Sofia. That defeat and the subsequent break up of the team heralded a boom time for the business of Dutch football. Since then, all the best Dutch players have ultimately sought to fulfil themselves abroad – Gullit, Rijkaard, Van Basten to Milan in the late 1980s bring us up to the present day – and the clubs persist in their belief that if a player wants to go and the money is good then go he must. Once the product has been developed and tested publicly before being marketed in the Ajax, PSV or Feyenoord shop window, then it is time to cash in.

Johan Cruyff, as gifted on the football field as he was vociferous off it, was the Di Stefano of his era, the fulcrum of Ajax of the seventies as the Argentine had been to Real Madrid 20 years earlier.

The beauty, though, of total football, and Dutch football generally, is that even the great and the good — even the Cruyffs — can be replaced. Admittedly not with an ease that means the team suffers nothing. But with a matter-of-factness that does not disturb the all important process of creating players from an ambitious Dutch youth. For Ajax, the permanent style is 3-4-3. And although the changes in personnel can be the difference between winning and losing in Europe, domestically, it is less critical. After all, PSV sell, and Feyenoord sell too. Domestically the playing fields are level, both literally and metaphorically. Remember, it's a business. And unlike the obsessed of Milan, and the passionate in Spain, that comes before everything.

The bonus is they come back. Because, after a while, a Dutchman brought up in a free environment grows to hate the restrictions of football abroad, whether it's Spanish claustrophobia or the Italian preparatory camps. Dennis Bergkamp, who made a troublesome passage from Ajax to Inter before absconding to Arsenal in 1995, complained of Italian ways: 'We in the north of Europe lead a very different life to those in the south.'

Ronald Koeman, sold by PSV to Barcelona, with whom he added a second

Ronald Koeman, like many a Dutch star exported for a large transfer fee, returned from Spain in 1995 to Holland. The next generation of footballers will benefit from the knowledge and experience he acquired in winning the European Cup with Barcelona in 1992. Koeman scored the decisive goal *(opposite)* in the Spanish club's 1-0 defeat of Sampdoria at Wembley, a fair return on the £ 3.5 million they paid for him in 1989.

European Cup winner's medal to the one he earned while playing in Holland, ended his exile in 1995 to play for Feyenoord. Thus the young will benefit from the richness of his experience abroad. Maybe one day, they will score the winner in the Champions Cup Final as Koeman did for Barça against Sampdoria at Wembley in 1992, as Rijkaard did for Milan against Benfica also before returning to Ajax. Van Basten, too, may return. After the 1995 European Cup Final, he was seen deep in conversation with Ajax officials, even though his paymasters Milan were themselves busy counting the cost of defeat. Van Basten to return? How inspiring for the young to learn from the man who contributed more than any other squad member to the Dutch success in the 1988 European Championships.

Justice delayed is justice denied. True indeed. Dutch success in the 1988 European Championships, staged in Germany, was only belated recognition for the great team of the 1970s, denied two World Cups. For many, it was too little, too late.

To appreciate fully this pain it is essential to spend a few hours in the company of any Dutch fan. Let him talk about Germany. Simply listen. There is no need to mention the war. He will. And early on. Germany occupied Holland for five years during a rather more serious European struggle between 1939 and 1945. They were not great guests. Relations have been strained ever since, and as they say in Holland: 'As in football, as in life'.

Losing to Germany in the World Cup Final in 1974 was a cruel blow for the Dutch. More so because their goal came from a penalty in the first minute after a move so sweet that no German had yet touched the ball, only for referee Jack Taylor to award one against them in the same half. But even if the events of 1988 were only partial compensation, they were a start. That year, referees were granted a universal pardon after a European Championships semi-final in which decisions went markedly in favour of the Dutch. In Holland, there is no such thing as an undeserved victory over Germany. So it was in Hamburg in 1988. Some justice at last.

The 1988 European Championships was the competition's first after the magic of Platini had established it as a rival to the World Cup. As always with Dutch football, the European Championships squad was far from united. Ruud

Holland successfully dealt with the challenge of Uruguay in the 1974 World Cup, but ultimately fell to Germany in the Final. Revenge eventually came 14 years later in the European Championships.

Gullit's presence in any camp generally leads to division. (En route to an away match with Milan, Gullit had to be restrained by team-mates from confronting the manager, Capello, on being informed that he had been dropped.) In Germany, even the responsibility of the captain's armband did little to temper his disruptive disposition.

Luckily, though, there were others of a less divisive nature. A calming influence – as well as an enormous talent – was present in the form of fellow Surinamese Frank Rijkaard. On being asked in 1995 what he would miss most in footballing retirement he mused: 'My shoes. I walk into the dressing room, look down at my

Frank Rijkaard's presence in the Dutch camp during the 1988 European Championships was a unifying one, compared with the disruptive influence of his fellow Surinamese national Ruud Gullit. The pair complemented each other further at Milan.

legs and see how they turn into my feet. I see my feet and my shoes. Shoes with studs. That is what I am going to miss.' Such a philosophical outlook helped take the edge off Gullit's prickly stewardship seven years earlier.

By 1988, Rijkaard was largely done with arguing, having left Ajax for an on-loan season in Spain after falling out with the then coach Cruyff. He later, like Gullit, joined Milan before returning to Ajax to nurse a young team to a European Cup; further proof of his capacity to bring fragmented individuals together as a team. Now retired, Rijkaard has set up as a clothes maker, producing denim underwear. Only such a phlegmatic figure could hope to market successfully such potential friction.

Although the team's third jewel, Marco Van Basten, usually stood apart – the classic centre forward's pose – he is nevertheless grouped with Gullit and Rijkaard to complete what many believe was the trio largely responsible for extracting revenge on Germany for the disappointments in 1974. Ask Bobby Robson about Van Basten and he can only draw breath: 'What can you say about him to a defender,' asks Robson, pondering possibly the words he uttered to Tony Adams before sending him out to mark the great man in the 1988 European Championships finals. Hardly a word, it would seem. Robson's team talk helped the England defence little. Van Basten scored a hat trick in a 3-1 win.

How could anything have stopped the man? Ray Wilkins once speculated that Van Basten had used a motorbike to escape the clutches of a defender so instant was his acceleration. Smashing speed indeed. His alacrity, too, in achieving scoring targets was no more than his early career had hinted. He made his Ajax debut as a substitute coming on for… Cruyff. A symbolic substitution if ever there was one. Van Basten's subsequent career, injuries apart, more than fulfilled his early promise.

It is amazing to think now that Van Basten struggled to make the starting line for the 1988 European Championships. Remember, Milan would in time consider him worth risking in a European Cup Final, when not fully fit, although he could do little to stop Marseille winning 1-0 in 1993. In 1988, he was as sound as a shire horse, just thought not good enough!

In truth, Van Basten was, at the time, more the thoroughbred about to win the Derby. With the benefit of hindsight, the 1988 series was probably his career peak, an assessment based on the number of match-winning performances –

three — he packed into the tournament. His efforts culminated in a stunning volley from an angle to clinch the Final against the old Soviet Union. This followed his massacre of England and a semi-final winner against the hosts Germany to make it 2-1 with only two minutes to go. Timing is everything.

Winning a penalty earlier in the game probably gave him more satisfaction, though. Remember the cruelty of 1974. Fourteen years on, Germany were leading from a Klinsmann 'earned' penalty when Van Basten fell over the outstretched German leg of Kohler in the box. Inga, the Rumanian referee, pointed, surprisingly — and it should be said, courageously being as it was in the partisan packed stadium in Hamburg — to the spot. Van Basten, who is reputed to refuse to speak German in interviews, said afterwards: 'Kohler caught me off balance, after which the referee pointed to the spot. And then I just had to bow to his judgement.'

Marco Van Basten's thoroughbred pose set him apart as a striker of distinction. He was too good for England, and the rest in the European Championships in 1988, and played a decisive part in three of Holland's five games.

The 1988 European Championships Final, the Soviet Union v Holland. Victory here, and the semi-final success against Germany, erased much of the pain of the previous decade's brace of World Cup disappointments.

How the Dutch laughed. All is fair in love and war and football, although there is little of the first when facing Germany. Holland went on to win the Final against the old Soviet Union 2-0. The combination of defeating the Germans and winning a trophy led to near hysteria in Amsterdam. Within 24 hours of the defeat of their arch rivals, a record had been cut featuring patriotic songs interspersed with commentary from the historic match. How they cheered when the commentator acclaimed Van Basten's goal, accompanied by a repetitive Euro-pop backing track. Sadly, expensive and classy football teams go hand-in-hand with tacky music.

The spine of Dutch football in 1988 – Gullit, Rijkaard, and Van Basten – became the backbone of Milan. It would dominate the Champions Cup as it had the European Championships. Their mastery of Germany continued in exile.

Inter had plumped for the vanquished – Matthäus, Brehme, and Klinsmann – as their foreign quota. As in Hamburg, the Dutch prevailed. The red and black colours of AC Milan blended well with the victorious orange on the streets of Amsterdam.

Although the *Guardian* is not noted for its achievements in tipping winners – aside from the day when the paper's racing correspondent, the late Richard Baerlian, advised his readers, 'now is the time to bet like men' on Shergar to win the Derby – it showed amazing foresight in 1994. Mark Fuller wrote of Ajax: 'With a smile he [Co Adriaanse, then director of training] drops the names of Patrick Kluivert… world class strikers set to emerge from the Ajax pipeline.' One year on, the very player came on as a substitute in the European Cup Final against AC Milan to score the winner.

With Ajax, though, you must enjoy the moment. Players move on. More than just the Milanese were watching in Vienna. Serie A in Italy may be experiencing some relative austerity – *Italia Paradiso perdito*, 'Italy a Paradise lost' lament the papers – but it remains affluent enough to tempt the majority of clubs beyond its frontiers to sell their best to them.

If Ajax do sell – and they have done so in the past – and the 1995 European Cup team breaks up, the wheels of Europe's most successful football production line may turn a little faster. Ajax coach, Louis Van Gaal, recovering from his exciting touch-line scissors kick during the Final that ended once and for all the search for the origins of Van Basten's technique, lamented on the rebuilding job he might face: 'I'll just have to start again.'

The task is undertaken in the knowledge that tomorrow's stars are close by. After all, more than half of the great Ajax side of the 1970s were born within two miles of the stadium. The ground they played in benefited then from the wheeling and dealing, as have the homes of Feyenoord and PSV. Because a good stadium means good crowds which means money to invest in the youth programme; which means the development of players; which means transfer income to buy star players like Ronaldo. Future Dutch success seems guaranteed.

GERMANY

'ARE YOU DEUTSCHLAND IN DISGUISE?'

Franz Beckenbauer, supremely gifted in his sweeper's role, was rarely rushed into error, whether he was wearing the white of Germany or the red of Bayern Munich.

'At club level and at the level of the national team, Germany is at the top. Maybe not number one, but definitely at the top. I think the Bundesliga is a true rival to Serie A. The league has improved from what it was a few years ago.'

When Franz Beckenbauer, the Kaiser, speaks. Europe should listen. But from what decade have these most commanding authoritative words of wisdom on German football been culled? The swinging sixties? Could be? (Germany were World Cup runners-up, successful club-wise in Europe). The seventies? Why not? (European Nations Cup, World Cup and Germanic Champions Cup victories). The eighties? Possibly? (more European Nations' honours, another Champions Cup win). The nineties? Can't rule it out! (the World Cup, again, European Championships runners-up). It is, in fact, a comment the great man uttered in 1994 on the return of Lothar Matthäus and other compatriots to the Bundesliga from the Italian peninsula after Italia '90. In reality, it could have been pretty much any time over the last 30 years.

How irritating. Not because of lingering wartime anti-German sentiment. No, the irritation is more likely to be, at least as far as the English are concerned, for the same reason that Arsenal only earn national support in European Finals when their presence means another UEFA Cup place coming England's way, and sees the accomplishments of Wimbledon acknowledged only begrudgingly by a culture that usually embraces such underdogs with relish. It's because German football is uninspiring and physically demanding. A bit like the British game. Only better.

Lack of flair, plenty of success; British international football also suffers from the former but endures a distinct lack of the latter. Jealousy causes British, particularly English, irritation. What hypocrisy! In truth the British should proclaim their Bavarian brothers as the master practitioners of the Anglo-Saxon game. But jealousy denies the opportunity to sit back and marvel at a job being done well. With some refinements — slow it down a bit here, a little bit of extra technique there — a superior product has evolved in Germany. Simple envy denies British fans the pleasure of lauding a European success story which, at international level, is without equal.

German football is an international brand leader, a product with a proven track

record, a commercial winner. Take European exploits. Germany has been involved in the decisive match in four out of the last six European Championships Finals. No other country can match this record. But then, not every country has taken the European Nations Cup as seriously as Germany, the true footballing multi-national. For some countries it is merely a pretty attractive warm-up competition for the World Cup. After all, the Home Internationals doubled up as the qualifying tournament for England, Scotland, Ireland and Wales in the early days. Only the old Soviet Union can boast remotely comparable achievements to Germany in this competition with one victory, the first Nations Cup in 1960, and three Final appearances, in 1964, 1972 and 1988. Germany succeeds because Germany cares.

But does anybody else? Some countries — or the individuals therein — see the European Championships as a distraction; a tournament that, if allowed to become an objective, will be detrimental to any attempt to win the World Cup.

Another German success in the European Nations Cup. Horst Hrubesch scores the 89th minute winner in the country's 2-1 success against Belgium in 1980 to further enhance what was already an impressive record.

Uli Hoeness misses the decisive penalty in the shoot out for the 1976 European Championships after 90 minutes and extra time ended 2-2 with Czechoslovakia. Had he scored, Germany would now boast a unique hat trick of successes in the competition. As it is, his country's record is still daunting.

How misguided. The Germans have shown it is best to work hard between World Cups. By doing so, they achieve continuity, blood youngsters and prepare for the other four-year party with hard competition. To Germans, success at any international level is the goal, failure never acceptable. Performing under tournament pressure and establishing the winning habit are essential for consistent success.

The statistics confirm it. Germany's detailed record (as West Germany until the wall came down, and united with the East since) would boast, had Uli Hoeness not missed a decisive penalty in the 1976 Final shoot out against Czechoslovakia, that they had played in the last six European Championships since 1972, winning three in a row and reaching the Final and the semi-final in the two others. And their World Cup form in between? Two wins and two appearances in the Final. So much for the suggestion that the European Nations Cup (which became the European Championships in 1968) is a distraction.

Soothing petty jealousy as it does, it belittles Germany's record to ponder on Hoeness' blazing miss in the 1976 Final with the shoot out at 4-3 in the Czechs' favour. But, the game in Belgrade against the surprise Finalists nevertheless highlights some of the reasons why Germany does consistently well in European international competitions. Against the Czechs, the Germans were in danger of being outplayed and went 2-0 down, but with Anglo-Saxon resilience, they clawed their way back into the game and drew level in normal time before playing out a goalless extra time. The Czechs were, most certainly, worthy winners, with the Germans under pressure for long periods, but only by the narrowest of margins.

Beckenbauer reflects: 'The German mentality is stronger than that of other nations. I can assure you Germany does not have better players, but even when they are under pressure they seem to maintain a winning mentality. It is not because Germans play better football.'

Arrogance and magnanimity in the same sentence. The Germans, masters of international football and usually, as is the case with Beckenbauer, a second language.

If you are a Bayern Munich player and you want to have a beer to go with your high energy pre-match meal, you have to be a full international. Baresi's commands Italian dinner tables by tugging on the captain's armband. Bavaria's finest pay greater homage to those who can doff an international cap. Achievements in international football rank higher than domestic accomplishments, the award of club captaincy included. Only a full international can contemplate the possibility of thirst quenching at gourmet club functions, something Graham Taylor might have pondered when criticising his own star man for 'refuelling habits'. Geordie, or no Geordie, play for Germany and you stay sharp, have parts refreshed that might not otherwise be reached and become 'No. 1' footballers. Probably.

German footballers are proud to play for their country. Proud to turn out in even the most inconsequential of European Championships qualifying games — and today there are many. And none more proud than those who play for Bayern Munich, a Bavarian club to its core, with fans who wear national colours underneath domestic strips. Of course winning for Bayern domestically is important – the odd European Cup brings a smile – but failure is relatively forgivable. There is, after all, a higher goal. In Germany, the domestic drive is different to the commitment self evident when Manchester United chase the highest honours. Unlike at Old Trafford, where international failure is felt less than a defeat on Merseyside, in Germany, parochial squabbles are never the be-all and end-all. Club football is considered the beginning of a journey that should end in winning international honours like the European Championships. For Germans, it's the beer talking.

Alan McInally was a most unlikely Bayern star when he joined in 1989. He is a Scot. That the ebullient striker (Aston Villa among other British clubs) became something of a cult figure – although his nickname, Big Mac, indicates German fans are no more original than their Scottish counterparts who called him

Alan McInally stretches for the ball playing for Bayern Munich. The club would also be prepared to go to great lengths for its players if by doing so it could improve their welfare. In all respects, little is left to chance when Bayern play in Europe.

Rambo – is testimony to his individuality. There was, in this case, room for an out-sider. Mercifully for him, he joined the club as a full international. No Scotsman abroad should be expected to go thirsty.

McInally, though, was a sideshow for the fans, something he readily admits. While he was there – and popular – Bayern were splendid hosts but remained busy with the job of developing players equipped to perform in the European Championships and maintain a tradition. Indeed, there were eight internationals playing alongside McInally at Bayern, who he maintains 'virtually represent Germany' being from the staunch Bavarian nationalistic heartland. And it was these players that mattered above all else, for the purposes of the club initially, and ultimately their country.

'The players came first,' recalls McInally, of his three happy years. 'And if you do well they will do everything for you, right down to putting in light bulbs. I have been on international trips with the full Scotland side when delegates and friends have got on the bus from the airport before the players have even been through baggage handling. At Bayern it was different. I remember an occasion when Karl Heinz Rummenigge, Uli Hoeness and other great former players were sitting at a table before a buffet supper waiting for the players to go and get their food first. The players are always looked after. They receive the most respect.'

And the most massages: 'In Germany, a massage is not a luxury, it is a necessity. It may not be important to have a rub before a game or after training, but it can be beneficial. When I was playing for Bayern, I'd be lying on my bed and and there would be a knock on the door TELLING me I was going to have a rub.'

From light bulbs to travel arrangements, German players are kings in the quest for European honours and in preparation for international honours: 'Wherever Bayern were playing we would step on to a plane in Munich and there would be a bus waiting for us – Spain, Finland, Albania – when we stepped off at the other end. And it was OUR bus. When we got home again, there was food and beer, everything we needed.'

Ah, the beer again, but not for everyone. The beer rule indicates clearly to every player that his ultimate ambition is to be in the national side. McInally relates: 'International football is hugely respected. You knew your place and re-fined your aims and ambitions accordingly. The rules bring a sort of determination with them. The practice games were never 10-8 but more like 2-1. Training was never a laugh. It was your job and you did it right. Training determined who played at the weekend and, like a lot of countries on the continent, there was no reserve team football.

'At Bayern, it's for the club but also for the country. If you played on Saturday, you trained on Sunday and you are monitored every day. I would weigh myself, not just at the beginning of the season but every day. They own you.'

McInally also knew his place. Big Mac or no Big Mac, he was, being Scottish, never any more significant to the grand international plan than accompanying fries: 'At the time there was a national campaign "Mein Freund ist ein Ausländer" [my friend is a foreigner] and I learnt German very quickly which endeared me to the other players. I was quite bubbly and liked a laugh. But, although there are foreigners in Germany there are not enough to affect [the quality of] the national side. The national side is revered. Whenever they play, the game is live. Wherever. I don't think a non-German has ever usurped the country the way Cantona has English players [as a hero]. Maybe the right person has not come along, but the population in Bavaria is predominately German. Mark Hughes, for one, came for eight months and couldn't wait to leave.'

Bayern only? No beer. German international? Cheers. One nation drinking together. The results in the European Championships speak for themselves.

Franz Beckenbauer – Bayern's most revered footballing son – believes the game is part of the national culture. He explains: 'If you are born in Germany, football is a tradition. It is a simple game, simple rules, you don't even need shoes to play. When I was young, we played barefoot in the street.'

He adds: 'Defeat belongs to life like victory.' One might be tempted to ask, bearing in mind the success Beckenbauer has enjoyed as a player and manager, how the devil would he know?

German clubs, though, have indeed endured plenty of life-enriching defeat in the European cups. The domestic excursions abroad in pursuit of European trophies have achieved only adequate results in comparison to the standards set by the national side. Borussia Dortmund were the first German side to win a European trophy, the Cup Winners' Cup in 1966, defeating Liverpool 2-1 in Glasgow.

Franz Becken-bauer, the Kaiser, who excelled with Bayern and Germany, is the product of a game that he believes is part of the national culture. His humble begin-nings included barefoot football in the street.

Bayern followed up with success in the same competition the following year beating Glasgow Rangers in the Final. But in the early days of the three European competitions, German clubs did not generally do particularly well. Nor since. They never have done, save for a brilliant treble of European Cups by Bayern.

The fact that the current Bundesliga only came into existence in 1963 is a partial explanation. Prior to that, the champions had been determined by a play-off between the winners of two round-robin competitions. German clubs were relatively soft compared with domestically-toughened Spaniards, British and Italians, being without domestic competition of the same intensity. With the invitation to 16 clubs to join the Federal League — and the creation of a divisional structure beneath — came some purpose to the league and greater resilience to the clubs. Nevertheless, this excuse apart, the overall record of German clubs in Europe is not great. It never has been. In the UEFA Cup, sporadic success, for Borussia Mönchengladbach, in 1975 and in 1979, and for Eintracht Frankfurt a year later, by then recovered at least partially from Real's soul-destroying demolition in 1960 at Hampden. Bayer 04 Leverkusen ended a barren run in 1988 winning the UEFA Cup on penalties, and both Hamburg (1977) and Werder Bremen in 1992, have won the Cup Winners' Cup. But there have only ever been two German Champions Cup winners. Hamburg (1983) and, of course, Bayern.

Bayern are the one true German success story in European club football. Their three European Cups – 1974 to 1976 – followed Ajax's total football, and although, by comparison, they may have lacked the fluidity of the Dutch, Bayern made up for it with steely resolve and their ability to cope with pressure. But in truth, it is wrong to attribute even this success to the Bundesliga. After all, the greatest achievers were just the national team in disguise (the beginnings of a terrace chant perhaps).

Beckenbauer attributes much of Germany's success at international level to Gerd '68 goals in 62 games' Müller. Likewise for Bayern: 'He scored the simplest of goals, not spectacular like Pele.' Simple goals, simple victories, yes, and with decisive additional – and usually match-winning – contributions from a host of internationals. Of the German Nations Cup winning side of 1972, Maier, Breitner, Schwarzenbeck, Beckenbauer, Müller and Hoeness were all part of the Bayern success story that followed. In truth, Germany won Bayern's three European Cups in all but name.

In fact, the shared characteristics of Bayern and the national side had an even firmer base than the transient presence of mere individuals. Indeed, it was highly appropriate – and inevitable – that Bayern became incognito club flag bearers in Europe for the national side. Bayern's assumption of quasi international status when the club was a home for Germany's Nations Cup – and subsequently World Cup – all-stars was its destiny. It is a status in keeping with the club's capital location in the heart of Bavaria (Bayern means Bavarian) and its strong Germanic traditions. This evolution from small time club – Bayern were a second division outfit in the early 1960s – to symbol of national strength was completed with the club's move to the Olympic Stadium in Munich in 1972. The venue for international heroics was their natural home.

Germany's… sorry, Bayern's first European Cup win — in Brussels in 1974 — was a long drawn out affair; the first requiring a replay. Like many rematches of mismatches, the second game, against the hard playing Atlético Madrid, proved something of a walkover — a 4-0 success — the Spanish team having been somewhat fortunate to have shared a 1-1 draw two days earlier, also in Brussels. Second time around, Bayern made their superiority pay. Juan Carlos Lorenzo, Atlético's controversial Argentine manager, conceded after the Final: 'Two days ago, the Bavarians were dead. Today they played like gods.' Against such divinity and denied the option in those days of playing for stalemate and penalties, Atlético's unholy rough-house tactics made little impression.

A riot in Paris after some controversial refereeing had gifted Bayern a 2-0 success against English champions Leeds United in the 1975 Final provoked more tangible outrage from the pundits and from the fans. Who knows what Jimmy

Gerd Müller scores for Bayern against Atlético Madrid in the replayed European Cup Final in 1974. Bayern won 4-0 having been held in the first game unexpectedly 1-1. Bayern were said to have played like gods in the second game to win by such a margin.

The triple European Cup-winning Bayern team was little more than the national team disguised in red, with Beckenbauer, Maier, Müller, Hoeness, and Schwarzenbeck, all part of Germany's accomplishments.

Armfield, Radio 5 Live's expert summariser in between selecting the England manager on behalf of the nation, would have made of it, had 'His Earthiness' not in fact been on the bench as Leeds manager instead of at the microphone that night. His eloquence, at this juncture as yet unbroadcast, ultimately proved useful though. At the subsequent UEFA appeal against a four-year European ban imposed on Leeds for the disturbance, Armfield's no-nonsense northernness was instrumental in reducing the ban by 50 per cent. Where was Jim when Mrs Thatcher stepped in after Heysel?

Bayern's third Final in 1976 was a much more orderly affair. French champions St Etienne were ill-equipped to deal with the by-now worldly Germans, and lost 1-0. The usually emotional Italian press, forming an unusual alliance with the

French against Teutonic interests, reflected poignantly on the game played at – how inappropriate when you think back to Di Stefano – Hampden Park: 'Professional skill had triumphed over amateur enthusiasm.'

Maybe a harsh verdict. The combination of the stereotypical German player – strong, fast, efficient, ruthless, a winner – and the odd gifted individual, usually steeped in experience at international level as well, is what raised the performance of Bayern above that achieved by other domestic rivals in Europe before or since. Of course, the great Beckenbauer – twice European Footballer of the Year – hogs the plaudits, and deservingly so, as the identikit player most managers yearn for in their team. An attacking-minded sweeper, what a cocktail. But that rare breed, the German maverick, also had his moment.

Moments to treasure. In fact, for a German team Bayern had a disproportionate amount of individuals – three. Paul Breitner, for one, never pretended to conform. Versatile to the extent that he could play in defence, midfield and attack, he, like many wandering dilettantes before him, ultimately found his spiritual European footballing home at Real Madrid. But not before achieving true greatness with Bayern.

Last to arrive and first to leave training, Breitner was no team man. Indeed, it was whispered around Munich that he sometimes departed after training and matches to escape his team-mates with such haste that his hair was still wet. The damp, dark-locked one nearly missed his finest hours, the 1974 European Cup Final, its subsequent replay and that year's World Cup when injured by a missile slung by a Swedish fan.

Breitner, though, was more David than Goliath, championing the cause of the political underdog. Justice was served with his recovery in time to play in both events. He believed in a more democratic approach to team matters than Beckenbauer, and his departure to Spain in 1974 was no great surprise. How the Kaiser must have chuckled when Breitner eventually returned to settle his differences and captain Bayern himself, autocracy hardly in keeping with his strong left wing views.

Different to Breitner – he didn't, after all, adopt a Vietnamese orphan – but no less individual was Sepp Maier in goal. A tremendous rackets player, tennis' loss was football's gain. Using the big head principle so successfully adopted

Although no team man, Paul Breitner was a crucial part of the Bayern and German successes of 1974 in the European and World Cup respectively. He left in the same year for Spain and Real Madrid, but returned to captain Bayern himself. In doing so he merely added to his already enigmatic reputation.

subsequently by the racket makers Prince, Maier would sport the most massive gloves to deny opposing strikers so much as a sneaking glimpse of the net, which in football, unlike tennis, is worth finding. Too much net was on show one night in Amsterdam when Maier performed poorly for Bayern in a European Cup game against Ajax. On returning to his twelfth-floor hotel room, the keeper threw his

Sepp Maier's distinctive style of goalkeeping was founded in gloves that presented forwards with a psychological as well as physical challenge when they were trying to score. Against Germany, few did.

clothes out the window. Thank goodness for those big gloves at breakfast the next morning.

Maier, at least was spared facing Bayern and Germany's greatest striker Gerd Müller. Müller himself plays down his own brilliance in scoring 36 times in European Cup games alone. Indeed, he offers some words of sympathy to goalkeepers:

'God help them,' jokes Der Bomber, a nickname from a less politically correct age. 'Often I didn't know where the ball was going so how could they? Hundreds of my goals were scored on the turn with only the vaguest sense of direction. I always knew the net was somewhere close but not which corner I'd fire at.'

On joining Bayern at 18, Müller was dubbed 'the weightlifter' as he was nearly

Gerd Müller, whose prolific goalscoring for both Bayern and the national team of Germany, played a huge part in the success in European inter-national and domestic compe-tition. After a troubled few years outside the game, he has returned to Bayern as a coach, shaping the club and the national side's future strikers.

a stone to the bad when he tipped the scales. When not playing he worked as a furniture remover. Later in life, Müller – his 62 caps having become something of a mixed blessing – shifted beer as easily and after drinking for Germany and most of the rest of Europe, too, it was really only Bayern's rescue act that saved him from an alcoholic end. He now works on the coaching staff. Who says Germans aren't big softies at heart.

So much for the German stereotype. At Bayern in the 1970s there were enough exceptions to the rule to create one of European football's most formidable club sides.

Bayern have not won the European Cup since 1976, and though international success soothes the anguish, it still burns up the club. Remember, Bayern are, after all, quasi international. Remember also that international football matters in Germany like nowhere else.

Even the carefree Scot McInally remembers on his arrival the determination that existed to repeat the triple feats of past stars. There is disbelief at the club that success has proved so illusive for so long, and the well travelled Celt regrets he was unable to achieve a revival to sustain the inherent belief in the club's purposes; to furnish the national squad with personnel and also to win itself. He, even in failure, suggests: 'A lot of Bayern players have that arrogance of winners. We played Glasgow Rangers in 1989 in the Champions Cup and no one mentioned the prospect of defeat. I was the only one who knew what Ibrox Park on a European night was going to be like. In the end, we won 3-1 and they all wondered what the fuss was about. Scots certainly seem to need to raise their game in Europe, but the Germans… There is a difference.'

Still puzzling to McInally – clearly infused with Germanic self-confidence from his stay, ended only by injury – was Bayern's defeat by the mighty AC Milan in 1990 in the semi-finals of the Champions Cup before their conquerors went on to lift the trophy, beating Benfica 1-0. 'I am biased, I suppose,' he admits 'but they got an offside goal in the second leg in a 2-1 defeat in Munich, and the pitch for the first leg at the San Siro was terrible. We lost there 1-0 to a Van Basten penalty and went out on the away goal.'

A lack of confidence was not to blame for the defeat: 'Even against Milan there was an expectancy. Bayern had been beaten only once at home for 12 years. A lot of teams were intimidated by the atmosphere inside the Olympic Stadium full with 72,000 fans.'

McInally is not the first Brit to leave Germany disappointed at failing to lift the European Cup. Although Hamburg achieved the goal subsequently in 1983, three years earlier, they were defeated 1-0 by Nottingham Forest in a pretty dreadful game for everyone outside the City Ground. Bad, too, for Kevin Keegan, who had joined the club after helping Liverpool beat Borussia Mönchengladbach 3-1 to win the trophy in 1977 – a 'calling card' to German fans pending his arrival. He departed from Germany three years later without restoring the balance.

To win the European Cup for Hamburg would have been a fitting way for

Kevin Keegan, successful for England's Liverpool against Borussia Mönchengladbach in the 1977 European Cup Final, but not for Germany's Hamburg *(below)* against Nottingham Forest three years later.

Keegan to end his stint abroad. After early difficulties, his qualities had eventually won over players and supporters alike. His achievements fully warranted Europe's highest individual accolade, the Player of the Year award in 1978 and again the following year. It had, though, been quite a turnaround. Keegan's stay at Hamburg had not been without incident. His first pre-season photo call with his new team-mates had very nearly prompted a return to Liverpool as Keegan's individual enterprise clashed with club policy. Hamburg wore Adidas boots and he, for a tidy sum, sported Patrick. A walk out was narrowly avoided.

Language difficulties early on — and consequently poor service on the field — meant that the Mighty Mouse Hamburg thought they had bought was rather timid. Everything came to a head during a match when team-mates and new star seemed hopelessly at odds with each other. Keegan blew. One punch thrown out of frustration at an opponent and he was off.

It was a blow for acceptance. Months later, after wholesale soul-searching, Keegan was the team's fulcrum. The European Cup Final in Madrid two years later was the culmination of a resurrected relationship. The Champions Cup beckoned.

Before the game Keegan manfully struggled to lower expectations cautioning against German self-belief. He reflected: 'On the night the team that has the little bit of luck, which finds its game earlier, will win. The one who hits the post and the ball comes out, whose players have a few decisions go against them, will lose it.'

And so they did with a goal, as Keegan mused they might, in off the wood-work. With such foresight, it is hardly surprising that Keegan belatedly succeeded in management with Newcastle. Indeed, he even suspected who might do the damage that night in Madrid in the absence of Trevor Francis, injured and denied the chance to score the winner for the second consecutive year following his strike for Forest against Malmö in 1979. John Robertson was Keegan's prime suspect. He was right. It was one of the game's most prolific smokers — more a day than games a season — who baffled them.

Keegan had predicted as much also before the game: 'I can't work out what his strength is because he has got so many. He doesn't seem quick, but he goes past players with speed. He is very skilful and gets into great positions. And when he plays well Forest score goals.'

One, in this case, was all it took. And, to use Robertson's favoured Scottish vernacular, a grubber (or daisy cutter), to boot. In 1979, Francis had hurtled into the shot putt circle at Munich's Olympic Stadium, such was his momentum after flinging himself at the ball to score the winner against Malmö. Despite a field athlete's physique, the rotund Robertson's more leisurely effort was hardly-Olympian but equally crucial.

Mercifully, Germany won the 1980 European Championships that summer, beating Belgium 2-1 in the Final in Rome. Even for Hamburg fans a satisfactory end to the season.

A Keeganless Hamburg made amends against Juventus three years later with another dour 1-0 win. Keegan, meanwhile, journeyed to Southampton and Newcastle before retiring to Spain and the golf course. It was only a call from St James' Park to enter the world of management that disrupted progress from tee to green. He holed out and packed his bags.

Such hole-in-one directness is unlikely in Germany. It is not that the budding managers of the future are more interested in emulating Bernhard Langer. It is just that it is preferred that they go back to school first. Managers in Germany usually have to qualify as coaches before applying for jobs and although internationals are allowed to begin their studies without working their way through a host of preliminaries, they still face exams – yes, written ones – after study and work experience.

At least managers joining the German footballing world since the start of the 1990s have begun careers in a league that is seemingly on an upward curve. Crowds are up – Bayern registered a seasonal average for 1994/95 of more than 54,000 – and there is a national enthusiasm for the domestic game. The financial troubles of Italy have benefited the Bundesliga like no other European rival.

Beckenbauer's opening comments in this chapter are in full agreement with those of others. Uli Hoeness, general manager at Bayern, where Beckenbauer (always the Kaiser) is now club president, argues: 'The whole of Italy is in total change at the moment and nobody there is able to pay the price for tickets to see something as simple as a football match. Italy is still the best, but with the money German clubs have at the moment... The German clubs have a big chance to be number one in Europe.'

Jurgen Klinsmann joined Bayern Munich in 1995 after spells in Italy, France and Britain. His and the return of other exiles to their homeland have strengthened the Bundesliga which is on the verge of a boom.

Klinsmann, too, returned from Italy via France and, of course, England. It is a trend that is gathering pace, particularly with the drift from the Italian peninsula. Stefan Reuter, of top club Borussia Dortmund, argues: 'Their return has

Burgeoning crowds in Germany are filling the nation's grounds to see many of the country's internationals who have returned from exile during the nineties.

strengthened the Bundesliga and they now know a lot of good things.'

Even coaches come, like former Juventus guru Giovanni Trapattoni (although he lasted only a season at Bayern). Beckenbauer explains that the league's affluence has enabled the Germans to improve their game by drawing on all the available talent: 'We know that the Italian style is to coach tactically, movement sideways and forwards. The German style is powerful, moving, fighting, more like the English game. That is why we hired Trapattoni because we knew he was one of the best and most successful coaches and exactly what we needed to give our players more tactical skills.'

As German World Cup winning captain Lothar Matthäus points out: 'The football life is well. The stadiums are full. We have the same atmosphere in Germany that they have in Italy.' Indeed they do, after a season when over one million supporters attended Bayern games, the first time a German club has achieved a seven figure turnout in one year.

Klinsmann described his return to Bayern as something akin to answering the call. The club's interest in him, he maintained, could not be ignored. Since then there has been some disharmony. On being substituted in the 2-0 win against 1860 Munich in only the fourth league game of the new season, he angrily

Lothar Matthäus, *(left)* successful captain of Germany in the 1990 World Cup Final, believes German football is thriving.

Captain Bernd
Dietz noisily
acclaims the 1980
European Cham-
pionships
triumph after
Germany
defeated Belgium
2-1 in the Final
in Rome.
Although the win
in Italy was their
last outright
success in the
competition, the
Germans are sure
to challenge
strongly, 16 years
on, in Euro96. It
was ever thus.

complained: 'It cannot go on this way. If I don't get the ball, I cannot do anything.'

But Bayern were stopped only by a tremendous Ajax side in the 1995 European Cup semi-finals. It will surely not be long before a German side succeeds in the European Cup. And that the strength of the Bundesliga will see the country assume the domination of the UEFA Cup enjoyed in the nineties by Italy.

And the national team? They'll probably win the 1996 European Championships in England — home to, but no longer master of, Anglo-Saxon football.

BRITAIN 1976-1996

LESSONS IN EUROPE

Phil Neal *(red shirt, far left)* opens the scoring for
Liverpool against Roma in the 1984 European Cup Final.
By this time, the club was the undoubted master of the
continental game. Although the Italians, playing at home,
equalised, success in a penalty shoot out assured the
visitors a fourth trophy.

In 1964, the coach transporting Liverpool, the English champions, entered a Scottish holiday camp for a break on their journey to Iceland where they were to play their first ever European Cup tie. Full of his usual bravado, manager Bill Shankly strode off the coach and announced: 'Liverpool Football Club, on their way to Reykjavik!'

'Well you're on the wrong road,' deadpanned a grizzled Scottish car park attendant.

It was to be the first of many deflating experiences the Anfield club were to endure on their European travels as they realised being Kings of England meant very little abroad. Even in Scotland. On and off the pitch they discovered European teams didn't always compete in the spirit and style to which they had become accustomed domestically.

On the field Liverpool and other English teams had to familiarise themselves with *catenaccio* and swan diving centre forwards. Off the field there were new disconcerting realities: car horns honking as vehicles circled the team's hotel at night; phone calls at four in the morning; knocks on the door at dawn; cold bath water; locked doors; erratic room service.

Tommy Smith, veteran ball winner of Liverpool's early days in Europe (and a European Cup Final goalscorer in 1977), recalls: 'Our idea of being good hosts was to look after the opposition and make sure every facility was available to them. But when we went away we faced constant problems all over Europe. Telephone calls in hotel rooms throughout the night, fans driving past and sounding their horns, two hour waits for cups of tea, locked windows and pumped up heating to make you sweat with thousands waiting outside to spit and shout at you as you came out. At the stadium, the dressing-room key would go missing, the showers wouldn't work and so on. We used to go on four-day trips for our early games in Europe. That soon became a late flight on the night before the game, eating on the plane to avoid the hotel food when we got there and we would fly out as soon as the match was over.' Learning the lessons of Europe.

European success for English clubs had ceased to be novel by the early 1970s – although Manchester United, relegation looming, might well have despaired that the club's achievement in winning the European Cup in 1968 was already shaping up to be the one off it remains today. No matter. A host of clubs had registered their own successes on the continent. No country could match the depth of England's accomplishments. By 1973, Spurs, West Ham, Arsenal, Chelsea, Newcastle, Liverpool, Manchester City, Leeds United, and, of course, United had all won trophies in Europe. Add Celtic and Rangers to the roll of honour and Britain was all-conquering. For Liverpool, though, winning was not enough.

To some clubs, Bill Shankly must have seemed almost greedy. The occasional success in Europe to supplement titles and trophies closer to home was sufficient for most, but wholly inadequate to satisfy the all-devouring ambition of Liverpool's manager. Two geographical footballing phenomena recur in Britain; the capacity of Geordieland to produce a steady stream of gifted footballers, and the capacity of the west of Scotland to furnish the biggest English clubs with fiercely competitive managers. Like Busby before him, Shankly fathered a club that became an institution and was anxious that it should conquer the continent. In fact, he wanted to dominate it.

It was a fitting succession. If Manchester had been Britain's most appropriate European pioneer, Liverpool was equally suitable as a base from which her citizens would achieve seemingly permanent footballing residence abroad. A port city, Liverpool was, inevitably considering it was a landing base for travellers from Ireland and the Americas, a mixture of cultures, and once again home to the same Catholic liberalism that had spurred Celtic to look abroad. Liverpudlians, like Mancunians and Glaswegians, had no fear of Europe, only ignorance of it.

They were, at least, well prepared for the challenge of European football at home. In Anfield, the club had a towering fortress from which to launch its assault. 'This Is Anfield,' says the sign in the tunnel leading to the pitch. Within a few years of concentrated European campaigns, the name alone was enough to intimidate. And in support of the structural ambience there were vocal contributions to make any opposition cower, first from sound, and then with embarrassment. The terrace humour was acerbic enough to break even the great practitioners of *catenaccio* from Italy. Visitors from Milan – Herrera's Internazionale – were some of the first from the continent to experience the special mix of aggressive ironies that emanated from the Spion Kop. That terrace was, itself, an indication of the battling instincts of Liverpool Football Club, named

The Kop, the atmosphere that made Anfield one of Europe's most intimidating venues and a complement to great Liverpool teams, who excelled both at home and abroad, shaped by managers like the late Bill Shankly *(top)* and his successors, Bob Paisley and *(bottom)* Joe Fagan.

as it was after a hill in South Africa where dead Lancastrian foot soldiers had shared an 'acre of massacre' in 1900 during the Boer War.

Despite this vocal encouragement it took the combination of success and failure to prompt Shankly into giving Europe the full benefit of his mastery of the game. In May 1973, Liverpool achieved its first continental success in the UEFA Cup as well as winning the league. The following season, upgraded to the European Cup they managed to make only the second round, succumbing, by the same 2-1 scoreline, home and away, to their perceived inferiors, Red Star Belgrade. Taken together, victory in Europe at the end of one season and defeat at the beginning of the next, Shankly – and his legendary boot room support team – concluded that what had been sufficient for partial success in Europe was inadequate for the ultimate challenge of the Champions Cup.

So the learning began. Shankly was to Liverpool football what Leadbetter has been to Nick Faldo's golf. Both are worthy of guru status; the former for devising a method that ultimately relocated the domestic centre of European football from Manchester to Merseyside; the latter for converting a Major winner into a major Major winner. Both recognised the need for strength under pressure; Leadbetter, for that putt to win the Open; Shankly for the last ten minutes of a European Champions Cup away leg – and eventually penalty shoot outs. Both had willing pupils.

Shankly began on a practical level. First there was an end to the misconception that European hosts provided a home from home. Lesson One over. Then came the tactical refinements based on the experience of defeat but also of victory. After Shankly departed, suddenly in 1974, having established the quick strike travel routine for Liverpool abroad, the boot room team of assistant coaches and reserve team managers – first in the form of Bob Paisley and then Joe Fagan – took over. The trophies followed, and the learning did not stop until 1985.

European tactics have always had the capacity to disorientate. Remember your first day at school or the arrival of a new teacher. European football can be like going back to the class room. Tottenham's first venture in 1961 featured an early playground mishap. Spurs found themselves 4-0 down against Gornik Zabrze in round one of the Champions Cup. They would pull two back before the final whistle and later trounce Gornik 8-1 at White Hart Lane in the tie's second leg but, instead of promoting celebration, the aggregate avalanche merely highlighted Spurs' naivete in the first meeting. The manager, Bill Nicholson admitted afterwards the gravest of European errors on behalf of the then all-conquering double winners: 'We were taken by surprise. After that we learned. We did our homework.'

Liverpool always did their homework. Veritable teacher's pets they were.

Alan Hansen arrived at Anfield in 1977 to strengthen a squad already good enough to have won the European Cup in May of that year. A key lesson of European football that had caught out Manchester United – rebuild from a position of strength – had already been absorbed at Anfield. Liverpool went on to master the rest of the rule book and ultimately added a few pointers of their own. Hansen, who would later become head boy, remembers those pointers set in stone.

Rule one: a European tie is not just another game. Hansen maintains: 'They were different from domestic games, because of the opposition and their different techniques, systems and styles. You never played any team from the continent that would play like a British side.'

Rule two: European trips should never be a voyage into the unknown, both on and off the pitch. Hansen, who along with the rest of the team left the holiday mentality at home for foreign games, recalls: 'I don't think we ever altered our style. It was the way that we prepared for games that changed, the way we learnt every time we went abroad; when we were defeated and even when we won. When we played in the early 1980s, every detail of the trip was sorted out. The preparation was incredible. Every detail, when we were going to travel, what we were going to eat – we took our own chefs, they prepared all the food – when we were going to train. We just learnt. They would look at every game afterwards and say what went wrong, what went right, what can we learn.'

Rule three: in Europe, which was, in Shankly's words, sometimes like the 'Battle of the Bulge', psychology is everything. Hansen confides: 'We always felt the first twenty minutes were crucial. Keep the crowd quiet, don't let them give their team any encouragement. We did it by keeping the ball. About ninety per cent of European teams would play with one man up front and they'd look to suck you

Bill Nicholson explains a tactical point to his Spurs team identifying a domestic rival's weakness. Preparation, however, let the club down in its first European venture.

in and hit you on the break but if you could keep hold of the ball like Liverpool could then it was not on. The continental crowds are a little fickle, more so than they are in Britain. That was why the first twenty minutes were so crucial. The chat was always the same: keep the crowd quiet and don't give the opposition the ball. If you don't give them the ball the crowd tend to get on the backs of their own team more than British crowds do. What it does also is encourage you, as it lifts you to hear the crowds get on your opponents' back. Little tricks like that helped. It was either sink or swim, you had to learn.' They did – to great effect.

Before 1976, English gusto had blasted its way to European trophies without one club ever threatening to adapt its style and beat the continentals with guile as well as gumption. Subsequently, some clubs had their moments. Some even learnt to the degree that Liverpool did. A double European Cup success for a relatively sophisticated Nottingham Forest in 1979 and 1980; the same trophy for Aston Villa two years later. But Liverpool evolved continuously during their period of study, becoming sufficiently learned in the art of the European game to dominate for seven years. Not since Real had there been one team so in control. They became as formidable – and mysterious – to Europeans as the continentals themselves had been to Liverpool during their sometimes painful process of European self-education. European nights at Anfield became an examination for the opposition. Instead of treading carefully on the continent, it was visitors to Anfield who tip-toed.

After their Champions Cup exit in the 1973/74 season, Liverpool spent future years accumulating knowledge and experience. The UEFA Cup was again won in 1976; a sign that the study was paying off. The following year a much revamped Liverpool registered a first success in the Champions Cup, beating Borussia Mönchengladbach 3-1 in Rome. They had improved enough to have mastered Europe's toughest exam.

It was deemed insufficient. Kenny Dalglish was added to the squad, along with Hansen, in preparation for the defence of the Champions Cup. Dalglish was ostensibly a replacement for Kevin Keegan, who had left for the continent and Hamburg. Just as the young Keegan had at Liverpool, so the Celtic buy learned quickly, adding to his knowledge of European competition gleaned from

Alan Hansen clashes with Real Madrid's Camacho in the struggle for the 1981 European Cup in Paris. Even clubs with such a strong European tradition were all the same to Liverpool who won 1-0, their third Champions Cup crown.

campaigns with Celtic. Indeed, possibly the only knowledge Dalglish didn't possess when he finally left Liverpool in 1991 was the name of an Anfield employee he for years mistakenly called Les. Appropriately, at the club where ignorance was the worst fault a player could have, it became Dalglish's nickname. Les' alternative sobriquet was 'superb' — a light-hearted jibe at Bob Paisley's frequent lyrical waxing over his Scottish international.

Superb nights were in store for new boys like Dalglish, the first of which will have satisfied the Kop's desire to match their Mancunian rival's greatest achievements. Liverpool were never driven to succeed in Europe with quite the same intensity that fuelled rivals Manchester United — although Shankly's competitiveness knew no bounds — but to win a European Cup in replica 1968 style at Wembley would, it seems fair to say, have featured high on the priority list at Anfield. They did. And Dalglish, even at this early stage in his English career a reluctant smiler, sported a grin that stretched from Wembley to Parkhead, the night Liverpool beat Bruges 1-0. He scored and had found a new 'paradise'.

The young Hansen earned his place in the starting line up at Wembley on the back of an injury to Tommy Smith (some poetic justice, perhaps, for the many walking wounded forwards who missed games through the hard man's 'enthusiasm' in the tackle). The aerodynamic kit Liverpool struggled to make fashionable in the late seventies and early eighties had yet to reach the tautness of European Cup Finals to come in Paris and Rome, but the red shorts at Wembley that night, nevertheless, offered only modest room for girth. Hansen, still slender from a Partick Thistle diet, slipped easily into his jersey.

For Hansen, a man who still remembers vividly Celtic winning in Portugal (he was twelve) the European Cup Final of 1978 was a dream. He also recalls (at least the early part of the evening) being at home with a six-pack in 1977, like the rest of us mere television viewing mortals, unaware that he was destined to play in the same competition within the year.

And of the Final at Wembley twelve months on? Hansen looks back: 'For me the place is unique. To play a European Cup Final there... I did not know what to expect. I remember sitting in the dressing-room before the game not feeling nervous and thinking that I felt all right and that I might enjoy it. Then out in the tunnel the importance of the game hit me, what had gone before in the history

Kenny Dalglish lifts the ball over Jensen in the Bruges goal for the winning strike in the 1978 European Cup Final, allowing Liverpool to emulate Manchester United's Wembley success ten years earlier.

of the tournament. I was a nervous wreck for ten minutes. But once the game started I was fine.

The game was not without drama, but never reached the heights that one might expect – we are eternally ruled by optimism instead of experience when it comes to the Champions Cup Final – of the occasion. The celebration of Dalglish after scoring the winner was perhaps the peak, a reminder today that, yes, he can grin for the cameras. The striker recalls of his deft chip over Jensen, the oncoming keeper: 'I must have been excited about that one. I jumped the advertising hoarding. Graeme Souness won a tackle and knocked it through and the keeper committed himself a bit early so I just lifted it over him into the net. The goal meant we won, but Phil Thompson made a magnificent clearance off the line just after that so it could have been extra time and who knows what could have happened then.'

What indeed? The previously unconsidered possibility of a flustered Alan Hansen, perhaps? His career path could certainly have taken a steep downward dive if Phil Thompson had been punditing on Sky that night! The man who ultimately shaped into the television 'Mr Cool' Thompson aspires to be, might never

Phil Thompson, backed by a relaxed looking Alan Hansen. The former's intervention on the goal line at Wembley in 1978, spared the latter blushes in his first European Cup Final.

have made it to *Sportsnight*. Why? Thompson's clearance was a product of necessity from Hansen's own back pass: 'I don't think anyone expected us to get beat and the Bruges team was not a great side,' says Hansen. 'I don't think they had a shot on goal until the last six minutes when I did a back pass and it was intercepted. The Belgian went round Clem [Ray Clemence] in goal and Phil cleared his shot off the line. I felt a BIT under pressure then.'

More was to come from the boot of Hansen, this time through kicking opponents; a variation in self-destruction on threading the ball into the path of opposing strikers: 'Two minutes after the back pass I nearly gave away a penalty, but it worked out all right in the end. If their guy had scored from the back pass and I had given away a penalty kick [why incidentally do Scots always call it a penalty KICK?] then there might have been a stigma, but it worked out OK. It was a great feeling going up the steps to the Royal Box.'

Hansen has few strong memories of Liverpool's two other successes in European Finals in which he played his part. He maintains, of the Bruges game, and subsequent Champions Cup-winning efforts against Real Madrid ('nothing special about playing them') in Paris (1-0) and Roma in Rome, that they were not, like most European Cup Finals, great games: 'Bruges wasn't a great game of football but then European Cup Finals rarely are. I never played in a decent one.'

Hansen does concede that the winning of a hat trick of European Cup winner's medals did have its high spots. Spots, like the one on which referee Fredriksson placed the ball for Alan Kennedy to strike the winner in the penalty shoot out against Roma at the Italian club's formidable home ground, the Olympic Stadium, in 1984.

By this time, their fourth Champions Cup Final, Liverpool had little to learn generally in Europe. But prior to the game Liverpool had ignored one of their most important rules; prepare fully for all eventualities. Following extra time in Rome, after a 1-1 draw, the shortcoming was laid bare. It was a penalty shoot out and, to make matters worse, the practice spot kick session Liverpool endured before travelling to the Eternal City had been the stuff of kindergarten.

Today, Hansen laughs: 'We had a penalty competition at the training ground before travelling, against the youth players. They got five out of five and our players missed the lot. Unbelievable.'

To Rome and not one of the young sharp shooting tyros in sight. Grobbelaar wobbled in goal to good effect and the rest muddled through to nurse the ill-prepared Liverpool in front. And so it came to pass that Alan Kennedy (who

Alan Kennedy nets the decisive penalty in the shoot out for the 1984 European Cup Final. He followed manager Joe Fagan's instructions to the letter and 'put it to the keeper's right'.

incidentally had scored the winner from open play against Real in Paris in 1981), stepped up to take what could be the decisive penalty, with Liverpool 3-2 ahead, having taken one penalty fewer than the Italians.

In truth, Liverpool had prepared perfectly, after all. Hansen relates: 'Alan Kennedy had missed four on the trot up to that point, all of them to the left of the goalkeeper. Joe Fagan, the manager, said to him: "Look son, if you get a penalty don't go to his left. You've just missed four like that. Instead of blasting it to the keeper's left try and place it to the right." And he did. Tremendous bottle.'

'It didn't matter a tap to us that we won on penalties,' adds Hansen. So says the man who admits he was the last person in the team likely to be asked to face football's cruellest torture.

Three years earlier, *en route* to Paris and Real, Hansen had enjoyed another memorable moment when Liverpool were drawn to play Aberdeen. It was an opportunity for the tall Scot to journey back home and show those with whom he shared a six pack on past Final nights, what a success he had become. Scottish bravado got the better of Aberdeen and the city's team paid for the enthusiasm of the local press. A full twenty-five pages of Aberdeen's evening paper were devoted to how the Dons would stage their own recreation of Bannockburn. It was, stresses Hansen, a big mistake.

'I don't think the English lads in the team could believe how fired up the Scots boys (Hansen, Dalglish, and Souness) were for the game. The paper fired up the rest of the team, too. We put up a great performance at Aberdeen, winning by a single goal, as they were a good side and I scored at Anfield in the return (4-0). It was really, really special. For some reason I was never a favourite at Aberdeen. They didn't like me. Even less than Dalglish.'

For Scots at home, the exiles' return to plunder would have been a most provocative and painful experience. For all the exploits of Celtic and Rangers in the late sixties and early seventies, it seemed the Scots lacked experience in Europe that night. Acquiring the necessary guile to mount a serious Champions Cup challenge could take years. Certainly, Liverpool's mastery of Aberdeen suggested as much. But over the course of the 1980s, the Scots did most certainly take heed, not least the vanquished Dons who took note of their brace of educational evenings with Liverpool. This coupled with the cumulative knowledge acquired over the course of six consecutive campaigns in Europe led to triumph against Real Madrid, no less, in the 1983 Cup Winners' Cup Final. An honourable mention, too, for Dundee United, UEFA Cup finalists in 1987 and European Cup semi-finalists in 1984. Lessons had been learnt north as well as south of the border.

In the European Championships, England have rarely excelled. Their greatest achievement in thirty five years – having qualified from a Home Internationals pool – was a third place in 1968, losing 1-0 to Yugoslavia in the semi-final in Florence. In the two-leg quarter-final, they beat Spain 1-0 at Wembley in front of 100,000 – and away by the odd goal in three with 120,000 in attendance. In the third place match Russia were beaten 2-0 in Rome. What memorable victories. Goals by Bobby Charlton at Wembley; Peters and Hurst in Spain and Charlton and Hurst again in Rome, actually. For the record.

Scotland qualified for their first European Championship finals in Sweden in

Although a full house turned out at Wembley for the Nations Cup quarter final clash between England and spain in 1968, the 1-0 win was a far from memorable triumph.

145

Aberdeen's experience of six consecutive European campaigns and a 5-0 aggregate defeat by Liverpool, taught them enough to win a Cup Winners' Cup in 1983. A proud Willie Miller holds the proof that they learnt their lessons in Europe.

(Left): Alan Hansen drives home a goal for Liverpool against Aberdeen, one of four on a special Anfield night in the 1980 Champions Cup.
(Below) Resplendent in their taut shirts, Liverpool celebrate a famous European Cup Final victory in Rome in 1984.

1992. In the absence of any minnows to upset the odds and humiliate a nation raised on World Cup embarrassments, they acquitted themselves quite well. They beat the soon to be disbanded CIS (the former USSR) 3-0 and lost with dignity to Germany and Holland. In celebration – and in recognition, perhaps, of a real collector's item, a Brian McClair international goal – one member of the Tartan Army was captured memorably on tv kissing a Swedish police woman.

Wales achieved a top European Championships rating in 1976 when they reached the quarter finals, losing to Yugoslavia over two legs, by a 3-1 aggregate. Many will remember more clearly the fashionable hose-pipe style red, white and green kit they sported than the crucial games, although a two-footed tackle by Terry Yorath during the campaign left a permanent mark.

Northern Ireland have yet to reach the final stages of the European Championships; strange considering their commendable World Cup record.

There is, though, one Briton who truly excelled under pressure on the European Championships stage. He is an Englishman who was, after a European Championships debacle, ridiculed to a degree that makes the opprobrium subsequently heaped on Graham Taylor for England's failure in Sweden 1992, seem a light load indeed. Four years earlier in Germany, the media even made news reports of the news reporting surrounding his exploits at the helm. Surely the possessor of England's broadest managerial shoulders, step forward Bobby Robson, the union's solitary Championship achiever – even if only for unprecedented restraint.

Under Robson, England travelled to the 1988 German-held tournament full of hope. False hope. They were comfortably beaten by the Irish (1-0), humiliated – remember how Van Basten turned Adams, almost screwing him into the ground – by the Dutch (3-1) and routed by the Soviet Union by the same score. In mitigation, Robson maintained it would have been different if England had scored. But, as the saying goes, 'If my Auntie had balls she would be my Uncle.' She hasn't. England didn't. And Robson was, in a manner of speaking, castrated.

How he responded. Robson's philosophical reflections on the very people out to bring him down were an education in restraint. As controlled as Liverpool's opening twenty minutes away from home. He once concluded after another withering assault following a poor performance: 'I accommodate the press, always have done, but they are very demanding, they all want a piece of the action. Journalism has changed. It has got a bit more vicious, more demanding. There are a lot of papers and everyone wants a scoop. There are two angles: good and bad. A lot of papers are happy to print the former and some want the latter. There are two journalists to every paper. The first writer covers the match and the second covers the dirt. It's junk journalism.' The concept of a circulation war mastered by a man at its very centre.

England's late arrival in Germany in 1988 – the last team in town, but not the last to leave – was inauspicious. The steps for their plane, wheeled out on the tarmac to allow the squad the luxury of disembarkation, went to the wrong aircraft. England would later be left similarly high and dry on the field. A training injury to Beardsley before the game against Ireland followed the runway misunderstanding. Lineker was unusually lethargic before the opener, and was later diagnosed as suffering from hepatitis. The expedition was worthy of the word ill-fated. It left the England manager, with a World Cup qualifying campaign ahead, almost broken. Beleaguered became Robson's permanent prefix.

Robson, though, like everything that is good about the English game, rallied in adversity: 'I will not let these people [the ones who had called him a PLONKER] get to me or rattle me. They have no qualifications. They have never been anywhere or done anything in football. Why should I listen to them?' Why indeed?

He went on: 'I will tell you who has the experience at international level: Ron Greenwood, Don Revie, Sir Alf Ramsey and Walter Winterbottom. And Joe Mercer, he had a tickle. They are the only ones who know about international football. And me.'

And on: 'We've had this strength of criticism, we had back-stabbing, the over the top media pressure. There is a time now when our players are going into some difficult [post Euro '88 World Cup qualifying] games. It is a critical time for national football. It is about time the country got behind the team.'

And on: 'We need two teams, one on the pitch, and one on the terraces. The media, television, the press, can either do a service to the game – they can educate – or they can brainwash.'

And on: 'I picked up a saying the other day. A person without public opinion cannot win, a person with public opinion cannot fail. We need the public with us.

Bobby Robson, who stood tall under a welterweight of criticism following the 1988 European Championships.

All the hullabaloo, all the unpleasantness, viciousness; it is time that it stopped.'

And finally: 'We don't half need the support. Without it we might struggle. I am asking the media to be fair and give us a chance.'

The same man, after Ipswich had won the UEFA Cup in 1981, 5-4 on aggregate against AZ67 Alkmaar, spoke emotionally about viewing the success of his team from the club's Amsterdam dugout for the second leg. He confessed: 'I have kicked every ball and headed twice as many as anyone else. When you set off on the management ladder you do not think about winning a European trophy. It is the thrill of a lifetime. It is the pinnacle of success for me.'

How Suffolk acclaimed him. The trouble was, however, that Robson was simply too decent for the subsequent scrap that awaited his elevation to national office. As an example of his priorities, the day news about his departure as England manager became public, Robson, with his home under media siege, still kept an appointment for a haircut. A HAIRCUT! Most would have been pulling the stuff out by the roots!

For calmness under pressure from an unforgiving media, Bobby Robson was a shining light in the otherwise dark history of England's European Championships campaigns.

Heysel, the end of an era.

Ipswich and Bobby Robson were just one of the combinations that achieved success in Europe, along with Liverpool's omniscient mastery of the European game. From 1977 to 1984 – apart from Hamburg's success in 1983 – the European Cup was won by Liverpool, Nottingham Forest, or Aston Villa. During this period, the Cup Winners' Cup fell to Everton in 1985; the UEFA Cup a year earlier to Tottenham.

It was unprecedented success in depth by a country. With English clubs, led by the example of Liverpool, at the peak of the learning curve and giving lessons throughout the continent, only an occurrence of wholly unnatural proportions seemed likely to bring an end to the run. Indeed, Liverpool were through to the European Cup Final in 1985, to play Juventus at Heysel, and Everton, as league champions, were already in the draw for the following year's tournament, boasting a side widely assessed as being capable of lifting the trophy. The prospects of a double handed Merseyside assault on the Champions Cup seemed good. Europe was in England's pocket.

Heysel brought to an end the sequence through an immediately self-imposed ban – upheld by UEFA – that subsequently ran for five years until 1990. The night in Brussels was a shameful episode, which saw thirty-nine deaths after rioting by Liverpool supporters. Remembering that for those thirty-nine who lost their lives at Heysel and their families who mourn their departure, consequences for football have no meaning, it is enough to say on the subject that English clubs missed Europe. Certainly more than Europe missed England.

Alan Hansen, who played for Liverpool that night in what must rank as the most irrelevant ninety minutes in the history of the game, has his football-related regrets as well, of course, as a heart full of condolences: 'If you have played in European Cup Finals, you miss it. You are playing against the best, and to win a Final is unbelievably special. Looking back, I think I missed out. I played in four Finals and after that I played for another five or six years. Looking at the teams I was with, I think I could have expected another two or three occasions.'

Hansen is adamant that the Heysel catastrophe could have been averted with better planning. He believes: 'A blind man could have seen there was going to be trouble. In Europe we would usually go out before the game to see our supporters and at six o'clock we went out. We had to walk past the Juventus fans. They were throwing bricks at us. They just picked them off the terracing. It was a volatile crowd. The fans were sharing one of the ends. Whoever thought that up ought to be put in a strait jacket. There didn't seem to be any control as to who was getting into the ground. There was bound to be trouble. If the crowd had been properly organised, Heysel could have been avoided.'

Little more need be added. It is only hoped that, just as Liverpool learned how to win European Finals, UEFA took note of how to stage them.

In 1990, English clubs returned to Europe. In the same season Manchester United won the Cup Winners' Cup in Rotterdam, beating Barcelona 2-1. It seemed to some that the clubs had never been away. Normal service would surely be resumed. A year before the ban for Heysel, in 1984, United had beaten the Catalans in the same competition, 3-2 on aggregate, clawing back a two-goal Nou Camp deficit at Old Trafford. Ray Wilkins recalls the game: 'There were 58,000 watching and we scored the crucial goal to make it 3-0. The atmosphere was tremendous. It was an incredible night. Graeme Hogg, a reserve player, was marking Maradona and never gave him a kick. It was fairytale stuff. To claw our-selves back from the dead against a top side with Maradona, Bernd Schuster and nine other probable internationals. Incredible.' Barcelona had been, according to Wilkins, 'mullered' – a wholly appropriate description for continental success bearing in mind 'Der Bomber'. Seven years on, such nights seemed set to feature regularly.

Yet in 1990, there was, once more, so much to learn again. Even for Liverpool, who, although champions in 1990 and eligible for the Champions Cup, were denied an immediate return. And for United, their earlier silverware notwith-standing. For all English clubs. And few, with Shankly dead and Busby long since retired, remained to teach.

It was like a return to the beginnings of Liverpool's campaign to dominate Europe. Many English clubs were starting from scratch. Squads, even those packed with international caps, were filled with personnel wholly unfamiliar with the game abroad.

Hansen, the ultimate advocate of a European education, argues: 'Playing in Europe is different, no matter how many internationals you have played. You take

(Right) Mark Hughes, scoring his first of his two goals, steered Manchester United to a 2-1 win in the 1991 Cup Winners' Cup against Barcelona, but in the Champions League three years later *(Below)*, the same opponents were overwhelmingly superior winning 4-0 in the Nou Camp.

Arsenal's durability proved good enough to beat Parma in one Cup Winners' Cup Final in 1994, cause for Seaman and Co to celebrate *(left)*. But the keeper's excellence was insufficient in the 1995 Final, Nayim's decisive long-range effort looping over his head in the last minute of extra time against Real Zaragoza *(below)*.

time to adjust, it takes a while to get used to the European game.'

Things, too, had changed. And were far from settled. A rule was introduced limiting the number of foreign nationals teams were allowed to field. The classification of the Home Countries players – Scottish, Irish and Welsh – as foreign hit English clubs hard. A Champions League was to follow with, by 1994, seeding for the great and qualifying rounds for unworthies to gain access to four leagues of four teams from which eight quarter finalists would be gleaned. There were enormous sums at stake for those who competed, particularly from television money. All told, the old Merseyside manual was of only limited use for the new challenge ahead which, after a five-year absence, was more akin to the new frontier faced by Manchester United over thirty years ago.

Hansen has thrown away his old European notes and made new ones on BBC pads. He believes the Premier League clubs representing England are low on the learning curve with much to familiarise themselves with in a short space of time, the foreigners rule not withstanding. 'In my day,' he begins, sounding a little bit like football's answer to Freddie Trueman, 'you did not get a second chance. The best Liverpool teams I played in were the 1978/79 and 1979/80 elevens and both of these did not win the European Cup. We had a couple of injuries and got beat in the first round – by Nottingham Forest, the eventual winners, and a year later by Dynamo Tiblisi. In 1994, Manchester United got beat 4-0 in Barcelona and were still in the competition. If we had been straight into the Champions League in the two years we were knocked out, we would, no disrespect to Forest, have won it.'

Bitter? Hansen supports his emotional reflections with some logic: 'English teams today cannot hold on to the ball, because to be able to hold it you need ten outfield players with the skill. Say your left back isn't good on the ball, the opposition just leave him when he is in possession so he has to play it long. Everyone has to be able to pass and keep hold of the ball. I don't think there is one side who can do it.'

Still proud to be a Liverpudlian, Hansen also rejects the notion that Liverpool dominated a weak European period for Italian, Spanish and German clubs. Liverpool, and other English teams successful in Europe, were a match for the best, he maintains. 'Only Manchester United fans would say we didn't beat anything,' he argues. 'If the Liverpool team I was in was in Europe now they'd have a great chance of winning the European Cup. When the going got tough we didn't fall apart. English teams have never been as good technically as continentals and, don't ask me why, but I don't think they ever will be. But English teams won the European Cup almost every year between 1977 and 1984 because they had good players, were good teams, were organised, played to good systems and when the going got tough, they didn't fall apart.' Shankly would have been proud.

Toughness, though, is no longer enough. The Cup Winners' Cup remains a happy hunting ground. Arsenal, winners in 1994 and Finalists the following year, succeeded using old values, combining them with newly acquired knowledge and experiences picked up along the way. But the Champions Cup? For that, according to the England manager Terry Venables, durability is not enough. He argues: 'Arsenal did it only one way – defending, defending, defending and hoping for a break which they got. They were never really able to push the advantage at home. They got through by playing away and counter attacking. There is nothing wrong with that as far as I am concerned but we have got to go on from there. We have got to be as slick as some of those foreign teams. We may win a European competition here and there, but I don't see us with the old authority in Europe now.'

The statistics suggest Venables has a point. In the five years since English sides, (indeed expanding the consideration to include British sides does not improve the figure) returned to Europe they have reached three Finals, all Cup Winners' Cup deciders. The comparable yield for 1981 and 1985 was eight, with only two of them in the weaker Cup Winners' Cup. Since Heysel; low on quality, low on quantity. Once again, there is a lot to learn in European football.

Terry Venables believes durability is not enough to dominate in Europe.

FRANCE

———

A COMING
OF AGE

Michel Platini, captain of the French team whose
performance in their home European Championships in 1984 gave the tournament the lift off it
had been needing since its inception in 1960.

Growing up can be a painful process. Teenage years are difficult; full maturity often elusive.

So it was with the European Championships. A drawn out adolescence, that began in 1960 with the inaugural competition, and which only came to an end in 1984 with the eight-nation tournament in France. Another fully-fledged adult footballing occasion was added to the world's sporting family of events, fully independent, if belatedly so, aged twenty-four.

Before 1984, half-hearted stagings, poor attendances, the odd quarter final walkover and more frequently, nondescript matches (particularly those qualifying games to which we attach so much importance today) had stunted growth and stifled development.

A European thank you, then, to France for winning with a side so gifted, a continent was inspired to emulate them. In the summer of 1984, the host's citizens maternally nursed their heroes' pursuit of the trophy until it was held aloft against the Parisian skyline by Michel Platini, captain of France. There, in the capital, the Nations Cup was confirmed as a genuine intermediary ambition to the ultimate football goal, the World Cup. Four years without the focus of a major tournament was always too long to wait for the cutting edge of true international competition. Thanks again to France, and also to Platini, scorer of nine finals goals, two hat tricks among them.

Without France the European football that transcends national borders so readily today might not exist. Just as Europe should ultimately be grateful to France, in the person of Gabriel Hanot of *L'Equipe* newspaper, for the idea of European club competition, so it owes her – and Henri Delaunay, secretary of the French Football Federation in the 1950s – a debt for proposing the European Championships as a test of international greatness for Britain and the continent. As Hanot was to clubs, so Delaunay was to nations. He was the brains and drive behind the international tournament. Sadly he never lived to experience the fruits of his toil. Perhaps, though, bearing in mind how long the tournament took to become truly established, it was better that he did not endure the frustration of seeing his baby struggle for air in the maternity ward of European football, already full at the time with the Champions Cup, Cup Winners' Cup and the still

Michel Platini fittingly holds aloft the spoils of French success in the European Championships in 1984 after his personal contribution of nine goals in five matches, including strikes in the semi-final and the Final.

mutating Fairs/UEFA Cup. The World Cup, too, seemed to monopolise the oxygen of publicity throughout the sixties and seventies.

It was indeed a long twenty-four-year wait for an identity. Consider its many names; today's self-explanatory billing, and before that the Nations Cup, the Henri Delaunay Trophy (still officially used), and in evolution the more mysterious Dr Gero Cup, the International Cup, and the Europe Cup. With so many titles, the European Championships has done its best to deny tradition. Ultimately though, the French took it upon themselves, when hosting the 1984 tournament, to finish what they had started and define the prize they initiated as one worth pursuing. They used the time-honoured method of winning with a team worth emulating. Just as the European Cup became the goal for all those who aspire to greatness once Real Madrid had triumphed, so the French, by succeeding so irresistibly, established the Nations Cup as an international event to rival the World Cup.

Consistent success, though, for France, reflecting the inherent talents of her footballers over the last forty years, would require their players to have defied a national sporting trait. French sport is not renowned for a win-at-all-costs approach, more a the-event-is-all enthusiasm. All games, however beautiful, seem to matter little to the national consciousness. France, the home of motor racing, has, after all, had only a solitary World Champion. Sport grabs the attention only spasmodically through heroes like Alain Prost.

It seems more important to the French that they are seen as good hosts. And they most certainly are. Some of Europe's greatest sporting challenges have their home in France; horse racing's Prix de l'Arc de Triomphe, cycling's Tour de France and tennis' clay court 'World Championship' at Roland Garros. But the public do not crave patriotic success with the same fervour that the British show at Wimbledon or the Spaniards showed in Barcelona for the 1992 Olympics. The racing fraternity of Chantilly embraced the British raider Celtic Swing, in 1995, when he had the temerity to skip his own Epsom Derby and win the French version in a controlled canter. Likewise, the foreign winner of the Tour, be he Belgian, Italian or Spaniard, is lauded.

French football stadiums betray the indifference. The hosts' homes do little justice to hospitality that usually extends to losing even more gracefully than the

British sometimes do. The club's municipally owned grounds are poor imitations of Italy's *calcio* palaces, themselves also dependent on public funding. Even at football's regular venue for internationals and cup finals, the Parc des Princes in Paris, it must share surrounds both cramped and unnecessarily spacious. While nobly named, the Park of Princes can hold barely 50,000, insufficient to house most national footballing passions. Moreover, rugby intrudes in spring. Because of this, football supporters must strain their eyes to see goals, as the oval ball game dictates a passion killing distance between crowd and action. So removed, love rarely thrives.

French football is a religion without faith, fit only for agnostics, compared with the devout of Italy and Spain. Ray Wilkins, who stopped off *en route* to Glasgow Rangers from AC Milan to play for Paris St Germain, relates of the capital site's biggest game of the season, when PSG clash with Parisian rivals, Racing: 'Our biggest crowd was 33,000 and that was for a derby. It is a bit sad as it is a lovely stadium.' The same stadium was close to capacity in June 1995 for Benfica and Porto, Portuguese immigrants to the capital flocking to see the play-off between the champions and the cup winners, in a charity shield style escapade replayed abroad. Manchester's Old Trafford three quarters full for City versus United but full for Real versus Barcelona? An unlikely occurrence.

In truth, there have been simply too many mergers, takeovers, relaunches and relocations involving important French clubs for Mediterranean and Lancastrian devotions to evolve and thrive. Since French football went professional in 1932, there have been a multitude of changes to the format of teams that today make up the French domestic championship. Each generation has its own truncated history. Indeed Reims, who contested the first European Cup Final in 1956 against Real, no longer exist. They were declared bankrupt in 1992 and thrown out of the league, leaving a city with neither a team nor a tradition.

Where is the soul? Reading and Oxford fought Robert Maxwell over his Thames Valley Royals scheming. In contrast, Montpellier's team is the product of a tranquil 1974 merger of Paillade and Littard; similarly Bastia Corsica (1978 UEFA Cup Finalists) was a merger between Sporting Club and Etoile Filante twelve years earlier. Toulouse also have origins in an amalgamation, of Red Star Paris and Toulouse in 1967, and, of course, Paris St Germain, was founded as recently as 1973 from the ruins of Paris FC and St Germain. PSG; hybrid European Cup semi-finalists in 1995. Hardly a basis for legend, with or without Ginola, recently departed for Newcastle.

Indeed, like Ginola, whose proposed transfer was as great a talking point around the time of the 1995 semi-finals as the games themselves, French players have not been slow to look abroad for more appreciative arenas. Kopa set the trend in the 1950s. He was already the paper property of the great Real Madrid when the giants of Europe beat his club Reims in the first European Cup Final. He gained a winner's medal with Real a year later. Platini, too, twenty years later, was forced to travel, for a Champions Cup winner's medal. He left European Cup Finalists St Etienne, who could not meet Real's ultimate challenge, for Juventus, who could. He maintains: 'When I joined St Etienne, the club was at the end of a glorious cycle in which they had won so much and the club no longer shared my lust for success. There was only so far I could go with them.' Determined, Platini continued his journey alone to Turin.

Eric Cantona also departed France having exhausted his options searching for a passion strong enough to match his own internal rage. He laments of France: 'There are players who as soon as the going gets tough, they get injured and yet they stay at the same club. They take their wage and do not give a damn.'

Perhaps only Olympique Marseille — the Barcelona of France — is built on a community spirit strong enough to survive upheaval and bankruptcy. But even down on the coast, the depth of feeling kept Cantona at OM for just a year.

In truth, when faced with football's ultimate European challenges, French parts perform disappointingly as if their sum will always be greater than the whole. Chris Waddle, who played for Marseille for three years, contemplated during his stay the apparent lack of team spirit: 'Even the French talk about their own mentality and say they are not very strong. Every time they get to the Final they don't win. They seem to become very individual when it comes to the big occasion. They get there by playing collectively and when they get there the team pattern goes. Maybe it is the glory?'

And so it was for Waddle and Marseille in the 1991 European Cup Final. For their poor full back Amoros it did indeed prove all too much. Waddle's former colleague was entrusted with a spot kick in the penalty shoot out after Red Star

Chris Waddle, an Englishman who shared in the French disappointment of another European Cup defeat, this time Marseille in the Champions Cup Final of 1991.

Belgrade had dragged out a scoreless 120 minutes in the hope of stealing victory in a sudden death climax. His team-mate relates: 'Amoros hadn't missed a penalty in his life. So he missed in the Final. He changed his mind. He used to hit them in the same spot, hard. Always. But that night he tried to place it.'

Such occurrences, though, need not be occasions for despair. Not for the French. Amoros can take a healing cue from Platini and his fond memories of the spoils of defeat in similar circumstances. Platini reflects on one of the cruellest of World Cup defeats: 'There are so many matches that I have won and lost it is hard to pick out moments. Perhaps the most wonderful experience, when we went through the whole gamut of human emotion – joy, violence, hatred, unhappiness, elation – was the [1982 World Cup] semi-final in Seville against West Germany. It was a great game which I was proud to be a part of, even though we lost, and proved that you can play football and have feelings.'

And Cantona? Like Platini, he believes: 'One day those who make football will have to understand that there is no salvation without the artist. Of course you have to win. But you also have to admit defeat so that football can again be a source of emotion.'

Le football c'est les plus beau des arts. What would Shankly have thought? Football, surely, is more important than life or death? Though not, it seems, in France.

Guy Roux has been manager of French club AJ Auxerre for more than thirty years. After defeat against Arsenal in the quarter finals of the Cup Winners' Cup in 1995, he pressed a bottle of the locally produced wine into the hands of the victorious caretaker manager Stewart Houston, and congratulated him. No doubt, he also uttered, *Bonne Chance* for the next round.

Roux did so with pleasure and with the safety of impunity. French football has never shared the English habit of blaming coaches for defeat. Platini, on his failure to secure as manager success for France in the 1992 European Championships, reflected: 'A failure? No, no you could never call me a failure because I am first and foremost a player. If I had failed in my playing days then I would agree with you but I am a winner. As a player, I never felt the trainer was to blame, if we lost. Likewise, as a manager, I never felt it was me who had won but the players.'

As manager of the national team, Platini advised: 'I ask the players to play and if we have to lose let it be against a good team.' Expanding on his philosophy, he adds: 'I need to ask my team to play to its strengths. The best players have quality. If the players are physical players, then they need to play strong. I don't ask them to play technically. If players are technical, I do not ask them to run, run, run.'

Tactics are secondary with this approach. Waddle maintains: 'I think they just pick the best players without thinking that hard about strategy, game plans, tactics. With some of the players they have had in the past, what else are they supposed to do? You've got to pick them really. But it may have left them sometimes a defender short at the back.' Indeed it may, but as Platini argues: 'When you are afraid of losing, you don't play anymore.'

On one occasion, though, French football possessed a fear of defeat because the desire to win, for the glory of France, was so great. So memorable was the experience, the waste of individual talent, the under achievement of domestic sides in European competition and the apathy and lack of tradition inherent in club football can be all but forgiven. French football may eternally disappoint, but how it thrilled, gloriously, in the 1984 European Championships.

It was said of the 1994 World Cup that only the stadiums contained the traditional fever that usually grips a host country's very existence when the greatest show on earth comes to town. To most of America, the World Cup may as well have taken place in another country. Ten years earlier, the threat of such indifference hung over the European Championships. It was only a shrug away. Platini was its salvation. Mercifully, the first game of the tournament – France versus Denmark – saw a strong performance by the hosts and their captain. A Platini goal clinched a 1-0 success and an apathetic public was stirred. Only a broken leg to Simonsen and the sending off of Amoros, struggling with the big occasion even then, blighted the game.

Amoros would return. In the meantime, Platini became the focus of both squad and public. BBC football commentator, John Motson, recalls his all-time favourite player: 'He had the whole repertoire; he ran so smoothly with the ball, had incredible vision and played with such intelligence. He changed the face of French football at that time. France had always been perennial losers but Platini inspired in them a will to win. With players like Alain Giresse, Jean Tigana and Luis Fernandez, he made up one of the most accomplished four-man midfields ever to have graced a football pitch.'

A mighty quartet indeed. Someone for everyone in a sometimes divided nation. Fernandez, the steel; Tigana and Giresse, together the industry and some guile; and Platini, imperious as a goalscorer or goalmaker – he boasts he could play in eight positions. The four encapsulated the diverse cultures of France's broadly-based population; Tigana of African descent (although he once earned a living making pasta), Fernandez and Platini, of, as their names suggest, Spanish and Italian origins respectively, and the stocky, powerful Giresse, uncompromisingly of pure French Bordeaux blood.

Tigana (below right) along with Giresse, Fernandez and, of course, Platini, combined to form one of European football's greatest midfields which also reflected the multi-cultural profile of France.

All for one and one for all. Inevitably, though, Platini annexed the bulk of platitudes. Like all European football's great combinations – pairs (Di Stefano and Puskas), trios (Gullit, Van Basten and Rijkaard), even elevens (Real) – the French midfield hangs best together, but Platini must stand alone as a goalscorer. His popularity remains enduring and transcended his chosen discipline. He carried the torch that lit the Olympic flame at the Winter Games in Albertville in 1992.

After the Denmark game, France was also ablaze. They ensured qualification

for the semi-final with a 5-0 thrashing of Belgium (Platini scoring three), and completed the finals group phase with a 3-2 success over Yugoslavia, featuring a seventeen minute hat trick from… Platini. Platini; seven goals in three games. Could there possibly be more to come from one man?

Indeed there was. And not just from Platini. In setting himself apart, he was joined by another. For the France versus Portugal semi-final was to be John Motson's finest hour. Listen to his semi-final commentary as at the end there is a definite quiver in his voice. It is entirely understandable as the venue, Marseille's antiquated Velodrome, built to stage games in the 1938 World Cup, was indeed an emotional place. After 'young' Domergue's opening strike – on his twenty-seventh birthday, how flattering a description – Fernandez twice, Giresse three times, Platini and Six all had chances, as the ball 'fizzed across the goal' and Bento in the Portuguese goal provided 'the acrobatics to deny the French captain', more than once. With Portugal's late equaliser came the gift of extra time, and with it great save upon great save, to go with a second strike for the guests and a Platini equaliser for France. 2-2. Then, with a minute on the clock, Motson's

'Platini, goal', so the French captain's greatest moment was greeted in the European Championships semi-final of 1984, France v Portugal, comfortably the tournament's best match.

Another Platini goal for France, this time against Spain in the Final of the 1984 Nations Cup, a recurring theme throughout the tournament.

moment: 'Tigana, two to his right, Platini through the middle. Tigana again, Tigana, Tigana, Platini, GOAL! Platini for France with one minute to go! It's 3-2! I've not seen a match like this in years!'

It was bad luck on the Portuguese to encounter a French team between World Cup semi-finals at its peak. Bad luck too for their Spanish neighbours in the European Championships Final in Paris. The Spanish themselves had been denied a home win in an international tournament – the World Cup – in 1982. Nineteen eighty-four was to provide no consolation, only a reminder of the incompetence of Arconada in goal, whom many Spaniards blamed for their country's failing in 1982 during the second phase in Madrid. For the opening goal in Paris, the veteran goalkeeper allowed a fifty-sixth minute free kick to slip from his grasp and into the net. Bellone removed any French doubt with a chip with two minutes to go. The opening goal had been Platini's ninth of the tournament.

What is left to say about Platini, other than the obvious; his goal tally remains an enduring record for the European Championships. The test of a great player is to win games his team would otherwise lose. On that criteria Platini earns, appropriately, a pass. Bobby Robson, who clashed with the French master when the 1981 UEFA Cup draw pitted Ipswich against St Etienne, is effusive about the very skill used against him in Europe: 'Platini could thread the ball through the eye of a needle. If you had three yards of space and he was thirty yards away he could put the ball exactly there. [He scored] great goals, headed goals, shots on the turn, shots on the run, angled shots, shots under the keeper. Aware of team necessity and got respect for it. Put his oar in. Marvellous in possession, always seemed to know what the overall picture was – and he could pass…'

Indeed he could. A lesson in winning with style was duly sprayed around the continent with accuracy. Sadly, Marseille, it seemed, missed the point.

In 1993 Olympique Marseille won the European Cup defeating Milan 1-0. They were the first French club to win a European trophy. It had been a wait of nearly forty years. Belated reward for initiative.

It had seemed, considering the talent, an extraordinary sequence of failure. In truth, the greatest let down ultimately was the apparent victory. The methods to

Olympique Marseille were acclaimed as the first French winners of a European Cup, beating Milan in the 1993 Final. The claim was premature.

which OM resorted in pursuit of a dream were indeed extraordinary. Financial irregularities unearthed sometime after the Final were enough to prompt UEFA to strip them of the title. The French football authorities subsequently traced other illegal payments and evidence that opponents had been paid bribes. Marseille were punitively relegated to the French division two.

The injustice of some defeats in football will always test ambitious men. For Marseille and the club's owner, Bernard Tapie, the defeat in 1991 against Red Star Belgrade on penalties had proved too disappointing an experience to take. Next time, Tapie, having seen that the vagaries of football could deny the best team the trophy, would leave less depending on the boot of Amoros.

Before Tapie, France had endured much European failure. St Etienne and Reims had both lost in the Final; the latter twice to Real, the former, in 1976, to Bayern Munich. The Germans proved simply too professional at the European game for St Etienne at Hampden Park. The 1-0 score line had a clinical ring to it, achieved as it was with the minimum of fuss. And Real? Well, in 1956 and 1959, Real had been Real, although Reims played well on both occasions. But don't French teams always? So it seems. Further text for the as yet unfinished book, *French Disappointments in Europe*, has been provided by Bastia Corsica, vanquished UEFA Cup Finalists in 1978, and Monaco, losing Cup Winners' Cup Finalists in 1992.

Even with Platini in their ranks, St Etienne were easily intimidated abroad. And not just by true pedigree Lions of Europe, either. In the 1981 UEFA Cup, good side that they were – indeed they won the competition that year – Ipswich Town were not Liverpool. Neither was the Portman Road swell possessed with the capability to break a side mentally, as the Kop had broken the steely peddlers of *catenaccio*, Internazionale, more than fifteen years before. No matter. The tie was lost before either team had so much as set foot into the European ring. Suffolk punch was enough to floor the French. In fact, Bobby Robson recalls that St Etienne were beaten before the bell.

'We were a good side, make no mistake. We won the cup that year, we were in great form,' Robson, pride still swelling, reminds any listener. 'But in the end, I think we frightened them. Every time their coach, Robert Herbin, saw us play we won. He came over to watch, we won, and played well. He came over again, we

Patrick Battiston *(long sleeves)* was part of the St Etienne side intimidated even before the kick off of their UEFA Cup quarter final against Bobby Robson's Ipswich Town in 1981. They lost 7-2 on aggregate.

won again and played even better, and in the end he said, "I cannot believe this team." He saw us play four or five times all told and must have gone back and said, "Jesus." He might well have worried his players. In the end we beat them 4-1 away and 3-1 at home.'

Tapie's arrival at Marseille in 1986 signalled a coming together of two parties who would not be so easily intimidated. The new owner's personal approach to business echoed the club's own motto, *Droit au but* (Straight to goal), which had rung hollow since Marseille were founded in 1899, denied the resources needed to compete with more affluent northern amalgamations.

Tapie's money – or more accurately, that of Credit Lyonnais, and others – soon changed that. His motives may have been manifold – he also saw the club as a direct route to Marseille city hall and a political career (he subsequently became Socialist Urban affairs minister) – but Tapie quickly rid the club of its reputation as simply a cup outfit. He tripled the club's budget turnover and purchased more than 150 players during his period in charge including some of the world's best. For the supporters and the city's population, Tapie's presence

Bernard Tapie, disgraced owner of Marseille, makes his views clear to coach Raymond Goethals. Tapie was a constant presence in and around the dressing-room during European campaigns.

represented a chance to hit back at the autocrats – footballing and otherwise – from the capital. For Marseille read Barcelona. For Paris read Madrid.

Tapie was a winner; in business, politics, life and so in football. The league title followed in 1989 (indeed they did the double). Nor would he be denied in the transfer market. Waddle came from Tottenham for £4.5 million. The figure is the one Spurs chairman Irving Scholar and manager Terry Venables agreed to quote to Tapie on the basis that he would not be prepared to meet such a demand. Tapie, though, had made up his mind. He wanted Waddle. The deal was done.

It was – Tapie and Marseille – a happy marriage, maintains Waddle. For the owner, both politically and business wise, and for the city, hungry for success and self-respect after many years of political and sporting subservience to Paris and the north: 'It gave Tapie a high profile. Owning the club was very useful to him. He would be on the front page of the newspaper every day.'

Of Tapie, Waddle also relates: 'He hated losing. He would want to win the toss of a coin. He did everything, bought players, was around the dressing-room before the game; very charming, very charismatic, very good company.'

And for a while, with Tapie in charge, the Velodrome was the place to be. The

Marseille players protest to the referee during their humbling of Milan in the 1991 European Cup quarter final, but there is little argument that OM, defeated in the Final by a negative Red Star Belgrade, were deserving of a European crown.

ground, once the venue for a French league match that attracted only 434 fans, became renowned for pioneering pre and post match entertainment. Fireworks filled the air after home wins. And win they did. Marseille made quite a bang.

In truth, though, the club was out of control. Prior to Tapie's arrival, OM had won four titles in an undistinguished history. During the same time, AC Milan, founded in the same year, had won more than double the number in Italy. Supported by funds from Tapie's own businesses and loans, many still outstanding, Marseille won the title four years in a row, from 1989 to 1992. The European Cup followed. Or so, at the time, it seemed. In the end, it was a grand illusion.

The sadness for Marseille and for French football is that the team was probably good enough to win the European Cup without having to break the rules. The team proved that, although investment in a generator would have helped to illuminate the point. On the way to the 1991 European Cup Final they outplayed Milan, the holders, both home and away, in winning a semi-final place *en route* to facing Red Star Belgrade. Only partial floodlight failure in the second leg in France cast a shadow over the excellence of the French side's victory clinched by Waddle's magnificent winning volley. A man more patient than Tapie could have seen that the subsequent defeat against the Yugoslavians on penalties, after a 0-0 draw, was only a temporary setback. For Marseille, the moment would have come. If Tapie had only waited, then Marseille could, like Platini, have won a European trophy for France.

Now Tapie has time to ponder. He was found guilty of attempting to bribe three Valenciennes players in order to rig a league match only days before the European Cup Final in 1993. Although he remained a Euro MP he began an eighteen-month jail sentence in May 1995, two years on from Marseille's second Champions Cup Final appearance. He complained on being sentenced: 'Now that the judges feel they have a free hand, I'll stay in prison for ten years.' Who knows how long it will be before a French club wins the European Cup?

In 1998, France stages the World Cup finals. Platini hopes that they will be a celebration of the game: 'I want 1998 to reflect my vision of football which is that football is fun. I want the World Cup to be a mega party.' Another 1984? Europe can dream. The French, too. Then they were both the perfect hosts and determined to win.

Who then will be great for France in 1998? Cantona? Certainly he is capable of inspiration. Already he has struck a chord musically. The Stranglers bass player Jean Jacques Burnel maintains: 'He has done more for Anglo-French relations than anyone since Brigitte Bardot.'

No more heroes? Many would agree that, because of Cantona's indiscretions, he doesn't warrant acclaim. Cantona, though, as rich in gifts as Platini, surely deserves the chance, granted good behaviour, to emulate his predecessor and honour the memory of 1984. As an editorial in *The Times* argued, to Cantona, football is more than, as Sir Thomas Elyot's *The Book of the Governor* claimed, 'beastly fury and extreme violence, whereof proceedeth hurt, and consequently rancour and malice do remain with them that be wounded'.

For Cantona, football is 'an art'. He expands: 'It is the finest art form because it demands spontaneity and most thought.' There is no doubt that his career is strewn with headstrong outbursts, most of them as difficult to understand as the various British pronunciations of his name. But, call him what you will – Contona (Eddie Butler), Can-toner (Ray Stubbs), Cantonaa (Barry Davies), Cantona (John

Motson, the most comfortable, naturally, with things French) the moment beckons. As it did for Platini. Fortunately for French hopes, both men enjoy an excellent rapport. The past – Platini on the bench – and the present – Cantona on the pitch – together in 1998? The French will hope so.

'Let us not forget that the place for an athlete is and always will be the stadium,' Cantona reminds us. As long as he doesn't stray, studs first, towards the seats again, the French may experience great nights in 1998.

Tapie, meanwhile, plans a screen debut on his release. He has been offered a part in a Claude Lelouch film, provisionally entitled *Hommes, Femmes, Modes d'Emploi (Men, Women, How to do it)*. The French – that fleeting moment in 1984 apart – more often than not the serfs of European football, are still the universally recognised masters of irony.

The 1998 World Cup finals offer 'Le Grand Eric' Cantona a stage on which to fulfil his and France's promise and potential as Platini did a decade earlier in the European Championships.

177

EASTERN EUROPE

MORE THAN
A GAME

Prosinecki converts his penalty for Red Star Belgrade
against Marseille in the shoot out for the European Cup
in 1991. Although a disappointing match, it, and Red
Star's Champions Cup campaign, was a perfect stage for
Balkans-based players seeking transfers to sample the
pleasures, footballing and otherwise, of the West.

Zvonimir Boban carries a photograph in his wallet. It is not the classic picture of a footballer's wife and children, the sort you might expect to find in the pockets of players, indeed the sort carried by people from all walks of life, all over Europe. It is a print of Boban himself, when he lived in Zagreb and played for the city's Dinamo team before the European transfer market took him abroad, ultimately to AC Milan. In the picture, his right foot, one of the continent's most coveted, has been caught a moment before it impacts on a policeman's skull. Boban admits: 'He hit me with his baton, but I kicked him in the head. His helmet came off and I just carried on kicking him. I was a man possessed.' A most candid confession.

The photograph records a day in 1990. Yugoslavia had yet to begin its final descent into bloody and all-embracing civil war but the conflict's frictions precede the moment recorded by the lensman by many years. The animosity between Serb and Croat is not a nineties phenomenon. The clash between Dinamo Zagreb, one of Croatia's strongest sides, and Red Star Belgrade, from the capital and the pride of Serbia, was always an occasion when behaviour reflected the shaky unity of Yugoslavia. That day in 1990, before the game, Red Star's supporters attacked home fans as expected. The police intervention was, as usual, a long way short of decisive in restoring order.

Boban recalls: 'I saw children being knocked over by Serb fans and I said to the policeman, "Can't you do something?" In those days the police were controlled by [Serbian] Belgrade and the policeman ran at me with his baton raised, shouting, "you son of a bitch, you are as bad as they are."' The rest was self-defence.

Bearing in mind Boban's current profile, it seems incredible to relate that the Croat, today recognised as one of Europe's most gifted midfielders, spent the next three weeks on the run in Croatia, seeking only anonymity and relying on friends and sympathisers for safe refuge. Then, his crime of assaulting a policeman carried a sentence of hard labour. Since 1993, his skills have flourished in the San Siro and now, with Croatia liberated and his own freedom assured, he reflects: 'If the Serbs were still in power I don't know what would have become of me.'

For Boban, football was his salvation. It has brought him wealth, the like of which the average Croat can only dream. Political changes in Eastern Europe have made it relatively simple for a player like Boban to leave his homeland for

AC Milan's Zvonimir Boban, a footballer whose experiences off the field are difficult for those in the West even to begin to comprehend, and which prompt him to divert some of his Italian riches back to his Croatian homeland.

the riches of the West. Clubs have been quick to tap the indigenous footballing talent of regions like the Balkans which have, over the years, produced some of the world's most gifted players, but in the past have been, for the most part, out of reach.

Today, European football acts as their shop window. Clubs from the West, some with ambition exceeding their resources, can ponder a region's previously inaccessible merchandise in the Champions, UEFA, and Cup Winners' Cups and also, increasingly as the political and national map of the mainland settles, in European Championships games. Transfer fees are usually cheap by domestic standards. The players in turn relish the prospect of earnings in hard Western

currency; earnings sufficient to provide for a high standard of living in the countries of their new clubs and also to meet the needs of families back home.

In Boban's case, as well as benefiting his family, a portion of the riches Milan
pay him finds its way into the coffers of local Croatian schools and charities.
Freed from the shackles of his homeland, Boban has found a worthy outlet for
his frustration.

Eastern Europe's first great team was the Hungarian national side of the fifties –
the Mighty Magyars. They drew enormous crowds wherever they played. A
curiosity surrounded them. And an edge. In 1953, England supporters came to
Wembley to satisfy the former and witnessed the latter. Led by Puskas, the visitors humbled the English 6-3 – England's first defeat, by non British Isles opposition, on home soil. The third goal, when Puskas dragged the ball back with his
foot, completely deceiving England's Billy Wright, generated a line of newspaper
copy almost as memorable as the exquisite skill. Wright, it was reported in *The
Times*, was, 'like a fire engine speeding to the wrong fire'.

After setting Wembley alight, they disappeared from view. Back to Hungary,
mainly to the army side Honved, where the government of the day decreed that
all the country's most talented footballers should play: Puskas, of athletic mind if
not gait; Kocsis, 'the Golden Head', and the equally gifted Czibor, all out of reach
even to the day's most intrepid newshound. Without the European competitions
of today, they were seen all too rarely. Blink, as Billy Wright did, and you missed
them.

The Hungarian uprising in 1956, against the country's puppet government, was
the death of the Magyars as a unit. If there was one justice that resulted from the
ruthless crushing of the people's popular objections that year it was that the
football team was abroad at the time. Many of the side preferred to remain
there, while uncertainty surrounded the fate of their country. In time, some
found clubs outside Hungary – or indeed, clubs found them. Puskas ended up
wearing the white robes of Real Madrid, alongside Di Stefano. His fellow inside
forward, Kocsis, also thrilled in the Nou Camp Stadium. For fans of Spanish football, it was indeed a bonus. The rest of Europe enjoyed more regular sightings of
other gifted Magyars, too.

In 1995, political changes have again effected a shake-up in European football. After the demise of Ceausescu's Romanian regime, the break up of the old Soviet Union and the fall of the Berlin Wall, a host of gifted players, who like the Hungarians might have remained out of regular circulation, are playing to a wider audience befitting their rich talents. The tragedy of Yugoslavia, too, has resulted in some of the most gifted players in the world, choosing exile to enhance their football careers. Their Mediterranean exploits provide some comfort in their troubled homeland. Small mercies.

Balkan brilliance, though, as well as Soviet excellence, is nothing new to Europe. Red Star Belgrade were, of course, Champions Cup winners in 1991; Partizan Belgrade, Champions Cup Finalists in 1966; Dinamo Zagreb, Fairs Cup Finalists in 1963 and competition winners four years later. The past exploits of Dynamo Tbilisi, 4-2 aggregate conquerors of Liverpool – defeated, not just beaten – in the Champions Cup in 1979, include success in the Cup Winners' Cup Final of 1981, a competition also won by Dynamo Kiev, in 1975 (helped by European Footballer of the Year, Oleg Blokhin) and again in 1986.. Dynamo Moscow also reached the Cup Winners' Cup Final in 1972. The roll of honour goes on.

The difference today is the availability of the same clubs' players. Before the upheaval in Europe, the governments and the clubs of the gifted did their upmost to retain as many of the most talented players, produced by their semi state-sponsored football programme, for domestic competition. The old Soviet regimes would deny a player the right to move abroad until he was in his late twenties or early thirties and had represented the national side on at least fifty occasions. It was a belated reward for service to the state. In other countries, like Yugoslavia, restrictions were less severe – a lower age limit on exports of around twenty-six was the norm – but they were no less rigorously enforced. And, even if a player was old enough to be eligible for export, there was no guarantee that the government would clear a foreign team's approach. Nor did the state have to explain its refusal.

Then down came the wall. Since the end of the 1980s, there has been a steady flow of players in their prime from the Balkans, escaping some of the strife and turmoil of the region, and from the old Soviet countries who have

Andrei Kanchel-
skis, whose
transfer to the
West at the age
of twenty-two
reflected the
political changes
in Europe in the
1990s.

been happier to grant players the freedom to leave because of the vital foreign currency their export has brought into developing economies. Andrei Kanchel-skis came from the Ukraine to Manchester United aged only twenty-two, perhaps the youngest Eastern European international ever exported. Unprece-dented liberties prevail in 1995.

The 1991 European Cup winning team of Red Star Belgrade – gifted indeed, although the Final, a goalless draw, did little to impress – is another modern example of change. Of the team that drew the sting from Marseille before win-ning on penalties, Dejan Savicevic went on to perform for Milan, Sinisa Mihajlovic departed for Roma, Vladimir Jugovic to Sampdoria, Stevan Stojanovic to play for Royal Antwerp, and Vlada Stosic to Spain for Real Betis (incidentally, Dragan Sto-jkovic, also formerly of Red Star, came on as a substitute for Marseille in the

1991 Final and now plays in Japan's J League). And there were others. Quite a clearout.

For those of the team looking to play in the West, Red Star's success was perfectly timed. Within two months of their success, the Yugoslavian conflict had begun and those who had been contemplating a move needed little added compulsion. Steaua Bucharest's appearance in the Champions Cup Final two years earlier was, by comparison, a shade premature for maximising export potential, but the team's success (coupled with a strong showing by Romania in the World Cup of 1990) proved enough, ultimately, to secure Gheorghe Hagi a ticket to Serie A and later the riches that come with playing for Barcelona. For the gifted of the Balkans, and others, the European stage has proved an ideal marketing platform.

Stojanovic dives to his right to save Amoros' penalty in the 1991 Champions Cup Final shoot out, a prelude to the keeper's transfer to Belgium, having displayed his prowess to a massive European audience.

Gheorghe Hagi, whose excellence in a Romanian shirt and for Steaua Bucharest, earned him transfers to Italy and Spain, and wealth beyond the imagination of many of his countrymen.

Footballers are a common breed. It would be flattering the players of Eastern Europe who have moved to Italy, Spain, Germany and Britain over the years to suggest that they have done so with the simple aim of becoming even more accomplished at their art. Sava Popovich, who has been one of the leading agents for players seeking exile from the Balkans over the last twenty years, concedes some of the transfers had their origins in financial envy.

Greed, though, has rarely been the sole driving force behind players' desire to leave behind families and friends and look for opportunities abroad. Eastern Bloc players have, after all, always been well rewarded at home relatively speaking. Often healthy ambition has led them to seek a move abroad, disillusioned with the domestic game. Ceausescu's insistence that the country's best players played for Steaua Bucharest, so that the team might score cheap political points by winning at home and abroad, left the Romanian league bereft of serious challengers to their supremacy. Corruption in East European football has distorted competition further. So great has the problem been for Russian football, the authorities delayed the introduction of three points for a win for fear that it might increase the less than subtle attempts – bribes – to arrange domestic results that have been a perennial part of the game. (It was thought that the greater points reward for a win would encourage small teams to accept money to throw games when the title race was at its hottest.) Great players are rarely content to have their gifts so belittled. Over the years, many have sought a purer challenge abroad.

Popovich, who brought Savicevic to the attention of the Italians, argues: 'It is true that some players moved through simple envy of Western players and the lifestyle of Italy and Spain, but the system, certainly in Yugoslavia, was different. If

Dejan Savicevic, sported the stripes of Red Star Belgrade before swapping them for the red and black of AC Milan.

say Hajduk Split or Red Star Belgrade wanted to sign a player from another local club they would give them keys to a house as the club owned many apartments. It was almost like an estate agent. If a player signed for four years he would get one and it would be his to keep thereafter. They would get a car also. If they stayed they would become privileged in the way that a footballer in Britain is privileged. It was a good life. People left for reasons other than the money. Some left because they wanted to be part of the big European scene. Red Star Belgrade have a great record in Europe over the years, but some players still wanted to play for the likes of Real Madrid.'

The patriotic instincts of many an exported player also weigh against accusations of greed. All the more so today. The changes in Europe have redefined the international football scene and have given some players the chance to represent their true nationalities, previously denied them by crudely drawn national boundaries. Attitudes to the opportunity suggest East Europeans have too much heart to be simply soccer mercenaries.

Alen Boksic, the Croatian Marco Van Basten (so dubbed after he helped Marseille beat Milan before moving to Italy), returns to his country, officially recognised by FIFA in 1992, to play European Championships and friendly games with a sense of pride greater than he had for the former Yugoslavia. He maintains: 'Now for the first time I am playing for Croatia, my country. When I played for Yugoslavia, it just did not feel the same. It was good playing at international level but it wasn't the same as playing for my own country. That drives me on more.'

His compatriot Boban who, along with Boksic, plays for Croatia at his own expense while the football federation gets its affairs in order, concurs: 'We never forget how much Croatia means to us. Before independence, we were never allowed to show our pride in the people. Now we have a chance to go to a football match and salute the flag that over centuries has been stained by the blood of our boys.' Pride enough to refute accusations of avarice.

He adds emphatically, directly addressing the suggestion that only money matters: 'We don't want money. Our country is the most important thing and if we can't go to war to defend it, perhaps we can do something more with our goals.'

The bulk of the 1987 World Youth Championship winning Yugoslavian team was in fact Croatian. Today, united under their own flag, Boban and Boksic enjoy

Alen Boksic, now based in Italy, returns to Croatia for internationals at his own expense, such is the strength of patriotic feeling surrounding the recently FIFA recognised country.

the best of both worlds; abroad in Italy, and internationally. Such things, like their talents, are hard to value. Even harder to nurture.

Some seasons ago, Arsenal were invited to Belgrade to play in a pre-season tournament involving the Brazilian side Vasco da Gama, and both Partizan and Red Star, fierce city rivals. On Arsenal's first appearance, it took only ten minutes before the watching fans began to boo. It was Willie Young, Arsenal's Scottish centre half, who was the subject of their derision. They had paid good money to see a quality match and many had never seen a player so clumsy. The following day's newspapers concurred and lamented how little talent such an important member of the great Arsenal defence had. Can it be possible that he plays regularly for such a prestigious team in the great English First Division, they asked?

Young's reception would be no different today. Changes to the political landscape, and an increase in the likelihood that the most gifted players will leave for foreign riches earlier than before, have had little impact on domestic football. For teams like Red Star Belgrade, the loss of individuals through transfers is of no greater inconvenience in the short term than previous bouts of injuries. The erratic demands in the past of the army have more than adequately prepared the old Eastern Bloc countries for prolonged absence of all but the most brilliant. The solution, a simple one, does not change. They just replace them with others, equally gifted, that have been nurtured for this very purpose. Very Dutch.

East European countries have never been short of raw materials. Clubs like Hajduk Split, Red Star, and Partizan, are as important to their respective communities as Benfica and Real Madrid are to theirs. Hajduk, a source of great regional pride, once supplied all eleven players for a Yugoslavian international fixture, and Red Star run over sixteen teams, excelling in different disciplines like volleyball, in addition to football teams for all ages. Sava Popovich maintains: 'If you stay at Red Star Belgrade you are almost guaranteed national caps and to become a legend.' As a result, young talent is rarely in short supply.

Red Star predate Ajax as European football's great producers of football talent. It remains the case today, with replacements both in number and in quality always in reserve to replace the absent or departed. Popovich explains: 'If Red Star begin with 3000 children in their youth programme, they will end up with 300 players and around thirty coaches for them. The process begins when they are aged eight or nine. Then there is no talk of tactics or blackboards. The children who are selected are chosen purely on skill, regardless of what position they might eventually play or if they are already showing signs of growing big and strong. It is more important that they can trap a ball. At Red Star they let them play with natural skills until they are at least fifteen or sixteen. Then they can get them in the gym and build up muscles and get out the blackboard to discuss tactics, but not before. It has always been the belief that players need to be of a certain age to appreciate tactics and to be able to cope with systems and be aware of team duties. The aim is not to destroy them at an age when all they want to do is play football. Everything else can come later when they are mature enough to understand.'

As a consequence, talent flourishes. In this respect, recent political upheavals in Europe have made little impact. At Red Star, it has been business as usual. It was ever thus. Popovich reports: 'When Red Star beat Liverpool home and away in the Champions Cup, both times by the same 2-1 score, nine of the team left at the end of the season; to the army, abroad, or to other Yugoslav clubs. But the following year, Red Star won the championship again by sixteen points. They always have six or seven goalkeepers on the verge of the first team so they can afford to lose one or two for whatever reason.'

The long term impact of the war in Yugoslavia on this process is hard to assess. Savicevic admits: 'The youth education system is not as productive as it was before. This could mean that many years will pass before a team from the area reaches the heights Red Star Belgrade reached in 1991. We had a great team who could have won many European Cups if we had stayed together.'

For the old Soviet republics, the future is even more uncertain. All players who previously competed in the Soviet Union have been given the option of declaring themselves available internationally for Russia, or for one of the revived Republics. Their decisions will go a long way in determining the respective strengths of the emerging leagues in the likes of the Ukraine, Moldova, Georgia, Latvia and Lithuania, established since the old Soviet Bloc broke up. Anyone with the foresight to predict the eventual shape of Russian football would be more profitably employed as a racing tipster. Perhaps the only prediction that can be made with certainty is that more players will follow Kanchelskis abroad.

Red Star's Prosinecki holds the 1991 European Cup, a triumph broadcast throughout Europe via tv pictures – a shop window for his talents.

If Europe's club tournaments have acted as a shop window for the the big Italian, Spanish and British clubs, then international football is mail order, with the catalogue, like a bulky Argos tome, hard to ignore. Trawling through European Cup Winners' Cup results may indeed be rewarding for a manager if video footage is available of the scorers listed. But, with preliminary rounds beginning in August, and matches in far off places, it is always possible that local television cameras will be occupied with other sports, and that feats of finishing will go unrecorded. Only the most determined search for action will be rewarded. International exploits, though, are more readily available. After all, every country has a national television station with resources to cover internationals. Indeed some players' agents mail film of their clients' prowess directly to managers in the West.

In the past, there has been no greater source of television footage than the World Cup finals and their qualifying rounds. Italia '90 and USA '94 produced furious post tournament transfer activity. The European Championships have never rivalled the World Cup in the publicity stakes. But after Sweden '92, there are signs that, particularly with the enlarged format, Euro96 will feature players who have maybe been denied recognition in European club competitions. Players who will grab the opportunity to display their skills to a wider audience in the hope that a good showing could produce a move. John Jensen's goal in the 1992 Final for Denmark against Germany, was instrumental in securing a transfer to Arsenal. The greater number of European Championship qualifying games can also serve to draw the abilities of a player to the attention of a club, dissatisfied with what is available on the domestic market. There seems little doubt that Sporting Lisbon's interest in Niall Quinn was sparked by Portugal's Euro96 group game against the Republic of Ireland. Quinn's club, Manchester City, have, after all, been absent from Europe for more than fifteen years.

Euro96 is the continent's first championship since mainland players began to enjoy greater freedom of movement. Coaches from all over Europe will attend the finals, having already cast an eye over countless qualifiers, in search of previously unconsidered talent. Only the most narrow minded manager will be absent.

After luring defectors from Eastern Europe perhaps the hardest job is keeping them happy in the West. Rumours regularly abounded that Andrei Kanchelskis was about to leave Old Trafford well before he did, to Everton in 1995. Such speculation will always surround the best players of a generation. Kanchelskis, though, did little to kill the gossip of a year before when he replied to a reporter's request to give, as a percentage, the likelihood that he would be departing shortly. 'Around seventy per cent' was his summation; in other words, more likely than not.

It was slightly misleading. The Ukrainian's response highlights one of the difficulties many players from abroad, particularly those from the East, will always have

John Jensen celebrates his goal for Denmark v Germany in the 1992 European Championships Final, a strike which drew the attention of Arsenal to his skills.

in adjusting to life away from the mother country; language. Kanchelskis later confessed to his interpreter that his linguistic knowledge of English numbers included one to ten, but then leapt to seventy. The limit of his vocabulary meant Kanchelskis's message was exaggerated. While the chances of him leaving Old Trafford at the time were greater than ten per cent, they were certainly not seventy per cent. Perhaps he should learn English for 'no comment'.

Language remains a problem for foreign imports. Kanchelskis laughs at his interpreter George Scanlan's dilemma when facing the task of translating the suggestion that an opposition full back is 'mutton dressed as lamb'. In Russia, the more common expression is 'a raven dressed in peacock's feathers'.

Footballers, though, have a way of adapting to change. But for East Europeans who leave for the West what remains constant is their undiminished status at home. Yugoslavia, having been thrown out of the 1992 European Championships, were readmitted to international football in 1994 and accepted an invitation to play against Brazil and Argentina in South America. A flight carrying the team and supporters landed in transit in Madrid where Dejan Savicevic joined the party having flown from Milan. On boarding, the Montenegran could only take his seat after shaking every passenger by the hand.

Today Savicevic, of Milan and Yugoslavia, has, like many others, the best of both worlds.

EURO 96
AND
BEYOND

BACK TO THE
FUTURE

Bobby Moore parades the World Cup after England beat
West Germany 4-2 at Wembley in 1966. The European
Championships in 1996 offers a new generation of
footballers the chance to achieve similar greatness.

On 30 July, 1966, England won the World Cup at Wembley. It was the nation's greatest sporting moment. Drizzle on a sun-kissed day produced a rainbow. Maybe, as folklore suggests, there was a foxes' wedding nearby, *The Times* speculated. 'Oh my, what a referee,' shouted the crowd, after a bad decision. (A refrain that has been adapted over time.) All the players were heroes, 'none more so than Bobby Moore as he drove his men on,' the newspaper recorded. What a day!

It was also Wembley's finest hour. *The Times* maintained: 'Never had the stadium itself provided a more emotional setting. From early afternoon the atmosphere was electric. It fairly crackled. The terracing was a sea of waving flags, the noise was a wall of sound that drowned the fluttering of one's heart. High in the stands there came the beating of a drum, a deep pulsating thud, almost tribal.' Wembley, home of legends, even then.

In 1966 the arena belonged to Moore: 'The stadium rose to the captain holding the golden, winged trophy in triumphant circuit. Honour and justice were done in that proud moment beyond many dreams.' English football's Golden Boy. How he is missed today. How his ambassadorial potential was wasted by the game after his retirement from playing.

The European Championships come to England in 1996. Who will be the nation's Golden Boy this time, drawn from a new generation? 'Will the play be as dashing, the gratitude to the England team as full and the tonic to the whole country as invigorating?' as *The Times* hoped, in 1966, future domestic international gatherings would be. Will it indeed?

In the summer of 1996, English football throws its biggest party for thirty years. Like all good parties, notification of arrangements went out well in advance of the occasion when tickets went on sale to potential guests for the thirty-one matches. Details of the entertainment were resolved over the course of 230 − more than ever before − smaller, one-off, qualifying gatherings between nations across the continent, between the autumn of 1994 and the following year. Catering and drinks will be arranged in good time. The hoped-for result? A sixteen-nation celebration of, specifically, British and mainland Europe's unique style of footballing excellence.

David Platt, who returned to England from Italy for the season preceding Euro96, the game's biggest sporting occasion in Britain for 30 years.

Of course, the World Cup remains unchallenged as the ultimate international footballing honour, but UEFA's doubling of the size of the European Championships' final format from eight nations in Sweden in 1992 means that the tournament has been given previously unknown depth. Now there is the chance for drama to unfold at a more leisurely pace, for themes to become established in commentators' and spectators' minds, for heroes to emerge – and villains to flourish – for more triumphs, and inevitably, more disasters to occur over three weeks instead of a hurried fortnight.

The scale of the finals tournament equals the 1966 World Cup. That year was the last time the nation has had to be so convivial to fifteen footballing neighbours, visiting in the healthy spirit of competition. In 1996, the English game comes a full circle since its greatest occasion thirty years ago.

Overall, the prospects for a strong European Championships are very good.

The World Cup has flourished as it has grown. Today perhaps only the Olympics overshadows it as a global event. Since the increase from sixteen teams to twenty-four in 1982 (a thirty-two-team tournament is just around the corner), the World Cup has become a tournament that can truly claim to encompass fully the area proclaimed by its title. So, too, the European Championships with its own expansion. The qualifying rounds for 1996 featured football on the continent's most far flung outposts. England's staging of the finals may mark a watershed more significant in the tournament's history than even France's stylish victory in 1984.

If the World Cup is an accurate guide, the main beneficiaries of the European Championships' overall expansion stand to be the emerging nations of Europe, many recently granted independence. In the case of the World Cup, the smaller entrants, gifted but inexperienced in the ways of international football, have

Euro96 offers Graeme Le Saux the chance to cement the reputation for excellence he has earned in the Premier League.

flourished given a greater opportunity to reach the enlarged finals and participate. The subsequent exposure to more refined technique has made developing countries more soccer streetwise. Zaire may well have been hammered 9-0 by Yugoslavia in 1974, and El Salvador 10-1 by Hungary in 1982 but such heavy defeats, reflecting a huge gulf in class, are rare today.

And, in the meantime, for the spectators, there is added drama almost guaranteed. A sixteen-nation tournament means, for the first time in the European Championships' history, centrally hosted quarter finals. Euro96 features more than double the amount of cup-tie knockout football than ever before.

For England players, the occasion is, as the World Cup was for Bobby Moore and his fellow squad members in 1966, a chance to claim greatness. For players like Alan Shearer and Graeme Le Saux, it is an opportunity to cement reputations, hard earned in the Premier League, at the highest level before hopefully

Euro96 gives Alan Shearer the chance to succeed at the highest level before the challenge of the World Cup qualifiers for France in 1998.

going on to perform in the 1998 World Cup in France. Opportunities, too, exist for the national team's management to prove that decision making and tactical awareness have improved since the country's failure to qualify for USA 1994. It is also a crucial test for those with ambition at Lancaster Gate for even greater occasions. The administrators of the English game have a chance to illustrate to the world that the only remaining international challenge after overseeing Euro96 – staging a second English World Cup tournament – is within the scope of the nation's football infrastructure.

Less romantic, but perhaps no less important, is the commercial challenge. The purists may deride the fact, but the Nations Cup is nevertheless, a welcome chance for the English game to make money to fund grass roots developments and future European Championships challenges. Related to this, although less obvious, is the musical challenge. Remember the impact of the vibrant combination of 1990 World Cup anthems, New Order's 'World in Motion' and Pavarotti's 'Nessun Dorma', on a nation's conscience? Such sounds may be an irrelevance to the grunts on the field, but the success of Puccini's score in particular, helped widen English football's audience in the years that followed Italia '90. Rumour has it that Oasis and Blur are set to team up and record a double A-side single for Euro96. A nation cocks its ears expectantly.

Challenges galore, then. And many spoils – money, knighthoods, chart slots – to those who successfully meet them. Indeed, English football has, as a whole, already benefited enormously from being chosen as hosts for 1996. In the way that Italian stadiums were extended and restored for the 1990 World Cup, so English stadiums have been upgraded with Euro96 in mind. While the clubs will, of course, earn a return on their investment during the course of the tournament, the improved structures will remain after the fifteen other competing nations have returned home. Future visitors to Elland Road, St James's Park, Anfield, Old Trafford, Hillsborough, Villa Park, and the City Ground, along with supporters of future cup final and play off teams who make it to Wembley, will consequently enjoy one of the benefits of Euro96 already banked well into the millennium; better grounds. In this respect, the 1996 European Championships have already spawned many a monument.

Leeds United's Elland Road ground provides a vivid example of some of the improvements made by clubs, principally to ensure their grounds would be granted Euro96 matches. The stadium is, after much investment, now a 40,021 all-seater, with the newly built East Stand, a home to over 17,000, all of whom are covered by one of the largest cantilever spans on the planet. The structure defies those who claim the end of terracing stifled the traditional atmosphere at English football games. In the past, few players relished their domestic visits to Elland Road – one of the league's most intimidating environments. The fans seated, it is still the case.

Elland Road, home to Leeds United and the impressive new cantilevered East Stand, concrete proof that English football has already benefitted from hosting Euro96.

With England booked into Wembley for the group stage and, whisper it for now, quarter finals, semis and the Final itself – regional football will nevertheless hope it has a lot to shout about on completion of Euro96. A successful tournament, nationwide, would add further weight to the argument that maintains the playing of all England internationals at Wembley is an anachronism. The evidence of the Elland Road experiment in June 1995 when England played out a 3-3

Umbro Cup draw with Sweden in Leeds, suggests staging of England internationals away from London's premier venue, has a future. The large Yorkshire crowd for the Sweden match compared with the small capital crowd for England's encounter with Japan at Wembley, in the same quadrangular tournament, suggests it would be a popular variation.

If the crowds are of good size around the country, it is then over to the lawyers. The contract Wembley has with the Football Association, guaranteeing it the right to stage all England's internationals at home, would have to be amended. Hopefully common sense could prevail and, if adequate compensation for loss of gate money was negotiated, some flexibility in scheduling could, post Euro96, take the national team to the rest of the country. Indeed, why should the national stadium bother with games like the Sweden match when the opposition were so under-strength as to be a pale imitation of the dynamic twenty-two who finished third in USA '94? Wembley should always be the home of legends – of the ghost of Moore – not mere substitutes.

On such matters, the committed and professionally involved will ponder. But so much for the long-term future. Of more immediate concern – what everybody really wants to know – is, can England win the European Championships?

Depressing as it is to accept the evidence, the simple answer, on past form, has to be, no. Yet the expansion of the finals format, from eight to sixteen teams, offers hope. England teams thrive in tournament conditions when the pressure is most intense. With this pressure, team spirit evolves and flourishes. Over the course of time shared in hotels, in daily training, at meals, the national team becomes a club side. Past eight-country tournaments have never lasted long enough for this to happen. That will no longer be true.

Bobby Robson, himself a victim of the sprint factor in past European Championships, argues optimistically: 'The longer England players are together, the better they perform. The spirit, the morale, it grows. One squad member might play for Manchester United, another for Liverpool, they meet twice a year and one kicks the other and the other kicks him back. Then they meet at an England squad gathering and they both think of their new team mate, "maybe he is not such a bad bloke after all". The longer England stay in an international competition, the better it becomes. Players trust one another and people see each other as reliable. The squad enjoys its own company. When I was England manager, there were little pockets who stuck together but they were never isolated from each other.'

The longer competition thus favours the hosts in 1996. Euro96 will, though, in all probability, go to the Germans. Their outstanding record makes them the historian's choice. All German national team managers, from Sepp Herberger in the fifties to Franz Beckenbauer, have won either a Nations or a World Cup (although Jupp 'I'll jump in the ocean if we lose to Algeria' Derwall took a World Cup soaking in 1982 dampening somewhat his Euro success two years previously). If past performances count for anything, Berti Vogts, Germany's current manager, is home and dry in 1996.

A safe prediction, indeed. What can also be argued with sustained authority is the European Championships will emerge much stronger after 1996 than at any time since its inception in 1960. Today, in the competitive world of sport, size is

Jan Eriksson scores Sweden's opening goal in their 2-1 win against England in the 1992 European Championships. England's future performances should improve with the tournament's expansion.

everything. Bigger generally means better. The chances of a side like Denmark achieving a surprise victory as they did in Sweden – having been eliminated in the qualifying rounds and brought in only at the last minute to replace the internationally disgraced Yugoslavia – and chipping away at the occasion's credibility are much reduced. The European Championships is now a tournament to be reckoned with. Future tournaments will not be taken by surprise so readily.

The delight Wigan experienced in dominating rugby league was not shared by anxious club chairmen who feared their monopoly was becoming detrimental to the sport's appeal.

In 1995, rugby league tore itself apart in an effort to embrace the continent and establish the framework for a European league. Those supporters who revel in the physical content of one of the world's toughest sports may have welcomed the infighting merely as an extension of popular on-the-pitch activities. But even in a discipline where competitors are renowned for their durability, the pursuit of a European league can, it seems, result in injured reputations.

The self-inflicted internal wounds – public accusations of treachery aplenty,

some verging on slander — were the product of a crude attempt to reform a league without consideration for decades of tradition. The major English powers in the code, alarmed by Wigan's recent near monopoly of the game's honours and the diminished spectacle provided, pressed for the extension of general competition to include the continent. Television joined them with the aim of bringing the discipline practised in the northern and southern hemispheres together. But the objective of creating a satellite dish spectacle to advance a European league, supported by television finance, was pursued by a determined league chief executive, Maurice Lindsay, in collusion with a number of the major clubs' chairmen, seemingly without any respect for history or community. Bearing in mind the swiftness with which a multi-million-pound deal with Rupert Murdoch's News Limited was agreed by the minority in power at the RFL, maybe it was inevitable that the heavy handed attempt to restructure clubs by merger, to fit a centrally conceived master plan, would end in the courts. It did. The grass roots majority of the sport saw to that.

To date, the development of a Champions League element within the European Cup has yet to produce the same levels of litigation. Less haste and a greater unity of purpose probably denied lawyers another money spinning benefit. Because its introduction was handled tactfully, the restructuring of the competition, begun in 1991, has not necessitated the possibility of creating new teams to make regional participation comprehensive. Nor were clubs with history asked to turn their backs on a domestic past and merge in order to be granted a chance to perform on European football's greatest stage. Indeed, by 1995, the Champions League seemed so much a part of the European scene, it was a feat of memory to recall time before it.

Perhaps this is because the Champions League has simply been a long time coming. In truth, the structure arrived at for the 1994/95 tournament was much closer to the original idea of European competition first conceived by L'Equipe's editor Gabriel Hanot and then adopted and nurtured by the likes of Santiago Bernabeu, father figure to Real Madrid. Although in 1991 it came with a rush, it was the culmination of forty years' procrastinating, not a few mad weeks of revolution.

The European Cup has always presented football administrators with

L'Equipe's Gabriel Hanot, a man whose vision was crucial in the establishment of the European Cup that has evolved into today's Champions League format.

something of a paradox; how best to arrive at a champion of champions without the time to stage the definitive league championship. A knockout tournament, while wholly appropriate for the Cup Winners' Cup – indeed, surely the cup of cups should feature straight knockout rounds without the home and away element? – asks those who excel at the league format to perform a different skill, that of winning cup ties. Likewise, the UEFA Cup.

When the idea of a Champions Cup for the whole of Europe was first mooted in the Parisian newspaper offices more than forty years ago, this paradox was discussed against the background of the existing regional tournaments of the day; the Mitropa Cup, for Balkan countries and some Italian clubs, and the Latin Cup contested by teams from the Mediterranean. In truth, the agreed two-leg knockout format for the new competition, which remained largely intact for thirty years, was a compromise. It was a muddled effort to try and ensure the best team had the greatest chance of winning, as in a league.

Over the years, by abandoning replays for tied affairs after 180 minutes, on the grounds of time and expense, the introduction of the away goals rule, and finally the spectre of penalty shoot outs, the competition became barely a distant cousin to the original thinking of Hanot, and Bernabeu, who always hoped for a European League, even in his lifetime. The introduction in 1991 of a league element – which by 1994/95 had become four groups of four, places for the winners and runners up in two-legged quarter finals, home and away semi-finals and a Final – brought some of the discipline of league football to the European Cup. It left only the anomaly of the UEFA Cup, with its league-determined qualification, and subsequent pure knockout format, to resolve.

Of course, money played its part in the introduction of a 'Champions League' to the European Cup. Lennart Johansson, president of UEFA, referred little to Hanot's aims when he justified the format of 1992/93; qualifying rounds, two leagues of four, and a Final. The Swede was neutral on the subject of history, preferring to concentrate on the financial benefits of the mini league series.

He said: 'The Champions League allows the eight best clubs of the year in Europe to benefit from the certainty of three home matches. This is naturally very important for their budgets, providing a guaranteed amount plus extra income [prize-money] for every point gained in competition. In addition it allows UEFA to provide much needed support for the rest of our membership. About eighty per cent of our membership is made up of small nations with small clubs. UEFA's share of the Champions League income means we can at last provide adequate financial compensation for those clubs who are always eliminated in the early rounds of all three club competitions. Not only that, but we can pass on extra financial support to the youth competitions. This is not the same world or the same game as thirty or forty years ago. UEFA has a responsibility to move with the times.'

With Hanot and Bernabeu's goal in mind, the historical irony of the last utterance was seemingly lost on Johansson. But whatever direction UEFA was moving in – in truth backwards – it arrived at an arrangement that has allowed the European game to flourish. The 1994/95 Champions League series, its dull Final apart, featured some of the best European football for many years with the league format justly determining who progressed in the competition. During the series, the penalty shoot out was redundant. Without the option of stifling opponents with a view to arriving at a sudden death lottery, play was more open. Indeed, the whole league format, in which a defeat, even at home, did not make elimination inevitable, meant attacking instincts prevailed over the cautious approaches of the past. The end, finally, of *catenaccio*, perhaps?

The experience of AC Milan in 1995 illustrates that the Champions League format is still far from flawless. To some extent, the demands of the mini league drained the former winners of any real chance of retaining their domestic title. The result of this was that after Ajax defeated them 1-0 in the Vienna Final, Milan, arguably still Italy's strongest side (the quality of champions Juventus notwithstanding), were consigned to the relative mediocrity of the following season's UEFA Cup. A Champions League, introduced to give the European Cup depth, will always be shallower without the likes of Milan, if their absence is largely a product of being asked to play too many high-pressure games the previous year. Likewise, from the season of 1994/95, the same applies to Bayern Munich, Manchester United and Barcelona; all deposed domestically while focusing on European honours early in their respective seasons.

Milanese schemers anticipated the problem. In mid season Adriano Galliani, vice president of AC Milan, approached Johansson with the proposal that the highest placed former European Cup winners in each country should be admitted to the European Cup, along with the domestic champions. Surprisingly, such a clause, if applied to the 1995 league placings, would have ensured Milan's participation the following season!

Before the rest cry 'fix', Milan can, at least, point to history in justifying their case. Early European Cups sometimes featured clubs, defeated in the quest for their domestic title, but accepted into the draw by invitation. A refinement to Galliani's proposal could be acceptable if the intent was to ensure a competition of the highest standard. Such 'fixing' may be too much for those who fear a European take over by the big clubs of the continent and Britain, but it would bring the European Cup even closer to Hanot's original idea. Think of the quality of the competition. Surely that thought makes further refinements of this nature worth pursuing.

With all this supposed prevarication, most people's idea of the villain of the piece is television. *The Times* newspaper, on the Monday after the 1966 World Cup Final, spoke in wonder about the 400 million viewers and the power television would wield in the future. How accurate. Today its influence over sport cannot be underestimated in light of what happened to rugby league in England. Many fear its disruptive potential; its lack of respect for history, the spectator and traditions. Once Murdoch decided to invest in rugby league, the very products he had in effect bought – the clubs themselves – became exposed to the threat of merger, largely against the wishes of many loyal supporters. Hybrid outfits were, after a struggle, avoided but perhaps not for long.

Television, though, is simply not powerful enough to make serious inroads into the footballing traditions of Europe. As long as, that is, clubs capable of domination do not become overwhelmingly greedy. It beggared belief to hear Franz Beckenbauer reflect in 1993, on Bayern Munich's failure to gain entry into the Champions League, that in some respects he was pleased the club was in the UEFA Cup as there was an extra round and a home and away final. 'You can actually earn more money than in either of the other two competitions, the European Cup and Cup Winners' Cup,' he reflected. Shame on the Kaiser. Most out of character. Mercifully, such unambitious attitudes are not common. For most, the Champions Cup is the goal.

Silvio Berlusconi *(left)* a man of whom football should have no fear?
He is unlikely to attempt to restructure the game as Rupert Murdoch *(right)* did rugby league.

True, the introduction of cup days – if it's Tuesday, it must be the UEFA Cup; Wednesday, the European Cup; Thursday, the Cup Winners' Cup – have been concessions to the broadcasting schedulers' demands, but most European clubs appear content with this and the level of remuneration provided by television. Moreover, television seems happy with its existing product, being party only to changes like the league format in the Champions Cup that have ensured a greater likelihood the best sides feature in the best ties, itself no bad thing. Silvio Berlusconi has yet to reveal himself as Rupert Murdoch in disguise.

As for television demanding the merger of clubs to enhance the competitiveness of the game, no such request is expected. Competition is sufficiently healthy. Even Milan in the nineties have fallen well short of matching Wigan's rugby league domination. Nor can the majority of clubs be bought by television with its pots of gold. In an attempt to smooth over some of the more over zealous restructurings of professional rugby, it was suggested that Murdoch's money would help ground improvements, much needed in the sport, and likely to be a major drain on future resources. By comparison, most football stadiums already adequately serve fans' needs. Many on the continent are municipally owned and well funded. Rugby was easy to bribe. In contrast, European football, not so. It should accept television's money when it is offered for a format that sits comfortably with tradition, and not fear the camera's influence. Nor should it fear the future.

It was written that the 'past is a foreign country, they do things differently there'. The history of European club football heaves with occurrences that refute the idea; that things and attitudes change with time. The European cups provide anecdotes over the years regularly recurring.

Take star poaching. In 1995, the giants of European football in the nineties, AC Milan, clashed with Paris St Germain in a much awaited Champions Cup semifinal. In the PSG line up was George Weah, the extremely talented Liberian, a potential match winner. Weah, though, had signed a contract before the home leg to play for Milan the following season.

So it was in 1956. The brilliant Kopa of Reims was part of the French side defeated 2-0 by Real in the first European Cup Final. The following year he

George Weah sported a PSG shirt in the club's European Cup semi-final against Milan in 1995, but the Liberian had already been promised to the Italians for the new season. Baresi, in pursuit here, would have to chase no more.

would play for his conquerors. It had been announced well before the Final that he had been promised to the Spaniards.

With both the 1995 and 1956 games being played in the French capital, historical comparisons are inevitable. Perhaps Weah should have chased and harried with greater enthusiasm against Milan instead of disappointing and fuelling innuendo and rumour. That, though, is by the by. After all, Weah's team-mates would have rumbled him soon enough. The general point is that transfers weakening the defeated and strengthening the successful have always been a part of the European game.

Indeed, it is usually the biggest names who are guilty. Before players were deemed as being temporarily cup-tied once they had played for one team in Europe, the German triple champions Bayern Munich, incurred general displea-

Terry Venables, entrusted with a nation's hope for the European Championships of 1996, points the way forward.

sure and accusations of malpractice after they signed Torstensson, a Swede, who had scored against them for Atvidaberg whom they defeated on penalties in the Champions Cup second round of 1973/74. Torstensson went on to play for Bayern in both the drawn Final against Atlético Madrid, and the replayed 4-0 drubbing. By his participation, many felt the spirit of the game had not been respected.

And so it goes on, controversies, among other occurrences repeated. More often, it is the memory of famous rather than infamous deeds that is stirred. But themes recur. Real Madrid back in the European Cup in 1995/96; the obsession of Europe returning to shadow Manchester United once again; another big star, usually Dutch, on the Italian scene, burdened with the task of collecting European honours by his compulsive president; a French disappointment; another Balkan discovery; a German Nations Cup triumph. But these are all, in themselves, part of one of the beauties of the European game; its enduring traditions. Rugby union is embarking on establishing its own European Cup while rugby league continues to stumble towards a European League. History shows which concept takes root more permanently. The quasi amateurs may lag behind their fully professional fellow oval ball exponents money-wise, but they have taken better note of the course, over forty years, of European football. A history worth attempting to emulate.

Euro96; football
comes home.

INDEX

BIBLIOGRAPHY

Glanville, Brian *Champions of Europe,* Guinness, 1991

Glanville, Brian *The story of the World Cup,* Faber, 1993

Hockings, Ron *Hockings' European Cups; who won what where when,* Mason, 1990

Inglis, Simon *The football grounds of Europe,* Collins, 1990

Kanchelskis, Andrei with Scanlan, George *Kanchelskis,* Virgin, 1995

Kuper, Simon *Football against the enemy,* Orion, 1994

Motson, John and Rowlinson, John *The European Cup — 1955 to 1980,* Queen Anne Press, 1980

Robinson, John *The European Football Championships 1958 1992,* Soccer Book Publishing, 1992

PICTURE CREDITS

BBC Books would like to thank the following for providing photographs and for permission to reproduce copyright material. While every effort has been made to trace and acknowledge all copyright holders, we apologise for any errors or omissions.

Allsport page 87, 90 (Clive Brunskill), 96 (Shaun Botterill), 97 (Dave Cannon), 99 (Chris Cole), 101 (Dave Cannon), 113 /Inpho, 125 (Shaun Botterill), 130-131 (Dave Cannon), 142, 154 below (Dave Rogers), 115 above (Shaun Botterill),157 (Clive Mason), 158 159, 171 (Shaun Botterill), 175 (Simon Bruty), 181 (Dan Smith), 201 (Clive Brunskill), 206 (Shaun Botterill), 213 (Ben Radford); Allsport/Hulton Deutsch Collection 19, 27, 56-57, 61, 69, 70, 74-76, 83, 116, 119, 196-197; Colorsport 13, 15, 16, 21, 22, 24, 25, 26, 29, 30, 32-33, 36, 37, 40, 43, 45, 46, 49, 51, 52, 55, 62, 71, 73, 80-81, 93, 95, 98, 102, 104-105, 107, 108, 110, 115, 117, 120, 122, 126, 127, 134, 135, 138, 139, 143, 146, 147 below, 150, 151, 154 above, 155 below, 161, 165, 168, 170, 173, 174, 177, 178-179, 184-187, 189, 192, 194, 199, 200, 203, 205, 211 left, 214; Steve Hale 147 above; Hulton Deutsch Collection 8-9, 39, 85, 94, 141; Popperfoto 63, 65,128, 211 right, 216-217; Press Association 145; Press Sports/L'Equipe; Sporting Picture (Uk) 169.

The front cover picture shows Dennis Bergkamp in action for Holland against Denmark in the 1992 European Championships in Sweden.

The back cover pictures show: *(top)* Ajax celebrating their 1995 European Cup victory after beating Milan 1-0 in Vienna; *(bottom left to right)* Nayim of Real Zaragoza with the 1995 Cup Winners' Cup; Lorenzo Minotti of Parma with the 1995 UEFA Cup and Brian Laudrup of Denmark with the 1992 European Championships trophy.